Additional Praise for

In the Best Interest of the Child

A long overdue guide to assist parents in minimizing the damage to their children before, during and after divorce. Children have only one set of biological parents and those relationships need to be preserved and supported. This book should be required reading before commencing divorce proceedings.
– George McLain, M.D.

Tells me *now* what common sense *should have told me* back when emotional trauma clouded good judgment. This is a parent's guidebook, especially for those too close to see beyond the parents' issues to value the child.
– Carole Balmer, Former Deputy Mayor and Committeewoman, Holmdel Township, New Jersey

Finally, a book with such a wealth of information and advice on such a huge topic relating to divorce, and written in a style that anyone in this situation can relate to. It is a "must read" for all family members involved in a divorce. It is both healing and enlightening! **– Robyn Mendez**, parent, Stuart, Florida

In the Best Interest of the Child

A Manual for Divorcing Parents

Nadir Baksh, Psy.D.
and Laurie Murphy, Ph.D.

Hohm Press
Prescott, Arizona

Cover design: Zachary Parker, Kadak Graphics, Prescott, Arizona
Interior design and layout: Zachary Parker; kadakgraphics@cableone.net

Library of Congress Cataloging in Publication Data:

Baksh, Nadir.
  In the best interest of the child : a manual for divorcing parents / Nadir Baksh and Laurie Murphy.
       p. cm.
  Includes index.
   ISBN-13: 978-1-890772-73-4 (trade pbk. : alk. paper)
  1. Divorced parents. 2. Children of divorced parents. 3. Parenting, Part-time. 4. Divorce--Psychological aspects. I. Murphy, Laurie. II. Title.
   HQ759.915.B34 2007
   306.874--dc22
                          2007022423

HOHM PRESS
P.O. Box 2501
Prescott, AZ 86302
800-381-2700
www.hohmpress.com

This book was printed in the U.S.A. on recycled, acid-free paper using soy ink.

11 10 09 08 07   1 2 3 4 5

*This book is dedicated to children everywhere,
who have the right to cotton-candy dreams,
and to their childhood, placed carefully
in their parents' hands for safe-keeping.*

ACKNOWLEGEMENTS

This book waited in hopeful anticipation that we, the authors, would finally hear the cries of the children, the real victims of divorce. We watched them over the years, tagging along behind their parents, sitting obediently in our offices, putting on brave faces while their worlds fell apart. Some of them, not yet school-age, seemed older than their years as they tried to come up with solutions to their parents' marital problems. Their parents, good, decent parents who would have laid down their life for their kids, were often lost, stuck in the quicksand of their failing marriages, blinded by their anger and rage, and unaware that their children were inadvertently placed on the marital battlefields, burdened by invisible scars. They confided in us, careful with their words, still trying to protect their parents in a convoluted way, not wanting to add to their burden. They bravely came forward year after year to tell us they were not all right; they were unable to sleep, unable to concentrate, unable to rid their minds of the worry that accompanies the unknown. Where would they live and with whom? How would they have enough money? Most of all, would they ever be happy again? These children, in their innocent wisdom, set the stage for this book to be written.

One by one they came, one by one they shared their stories, each with a voice that was barely a whisper, but in numbers grew audible, guiding our hands as we penned our book, their pleadings growing louder still as they reached Hohm Press, who marched along with us, in our journey to reach their parents and remind them of their promise to protect their children.

Many thanks to the Hohm Press team for their tireless efforts and creativity, and most especially our editor, Regina Sara

Ryan, for sharing our belief that we can all make a difference, one child at a time.

We thank our families for always being there with encouragement and enthusiasm as we reached the finish line. Our friends have endured our endless obsessions and fantasies with smiles and support, secretly thankful, we're sure, that our project is completed.

Mostly, we thank Divine Intervention, who always places you where you need to be, when you need to be there, and moves you forward even when you feel like standing still.

CONTENTS

CHAPTER ONE

IN THE BEST INTEREST OF THE CHILD

If you are reading this book, your marriage is over. Even if you're only mulling over the thought of divorce, trying it on for size to see how it fits, your marriage for all practical purposes is over. Divorce is a life-changing event, but so is the road upon which you are about to embark called single parenting. This road is unyielding and unforgiving; it is essential that you make no errors in parenting during and after your divorce if you want your children to be emotionally healthy.

It is not a random guess that you have been riding a roller coaster of emotions that has affected not only you but every member of your household in one way or another. Emotions, in their place, are wonderful, ingenious, and often involuntary windows into the recesses of our souls, but left to their own devices they can cause unimaginable damage and chaos. During the divorce process we will certainly deal with all of your emotions, including anger, sorrow, betrayal and loss, but there is another aspect to deal with, one which becomes equally important, that being the business aspect, or those decisions which will ensure your financial security and carve out the relationship you ultimately have with your spouse. We must combine the business aspect with the emotional aspect of this uncharted territory if we are to steer you away from the path of family dysfunction.

Divorce is not always a time when intelligence and common sense rule. Regardless of how sensibly you have behaved in the past, divorce is a time when you may feel surreal, as if the events that are occurring are happening without your input or control. If you allow your focus to blur into chaos and turmoil, you will do yourself and your children a great disservice.

Our belief is simple. Although it may not seem the case at this moment, be assured that you will survive the divorce regardless of the financial cost and the emotional toll. Your life is already taking on a new shape and will slowly rebuild itself. Often, what initially seems like an ending is really just a new and better beginning. Your children, however, may not be able to look ahead to that same happy ending. Things will not fall into place for them without a strategic plan for how to protect and preserve their emotional health and well-being. This plan should be drafted by you and your former spouse. Without it, your children's lives will quickly stagnate or suffocate in the mire and muck created by spousal mudslinging and attorney posturing. Our approach and answer to this quagmire is to focus on child-centered needs based upon their ages, intellect and emotions. In other words, regardless of your immediate needs, their needs come first. If this statement offends you, if you are reluctant or resistant to identifying and addressing your children's needs primarily and continuously, then you are going to have parenting problems.

Let's face it. Isn't the health and well-being of your children what you really want? To enrich their lives and shelter them from all harm? Of course. Then let's be clear. Although you didn't set out to cause them damage, your divorce, if not handled properly, will absolutely damage them and cause them anguish. To be clear in our mission to get things right in your family, we have an obligation to speak to you in direct fashion, without the sugarcoated style that many other divorce books offer because they don't want to offend anyone. We are not afraid to take a stand. In fact, we believe it is our duty to underscore the needs of your children so they don't get lost or disappear underneath legal paperwork. From this moment forward there will be consequences for every single error in judgment you make. The directives we suggest will be simple and concise so you can avoid costly emotional missteps because, frankly, there is no room for error.

Let's agree on a few more things. First, please understand that your children cannot function without you. They are not self-sufficient mini-versions of adults, and they do not have the intellectual sophistication to act independently. Regardless of their ages, they need you to be available and present, which does not mean just being a physical body in a room. It means you must be available to meet their needs and understand the milestones of their development regardless of the battles that are raging in your marriage.

You may be struggling, but that is of little consequence in comparison to the struggles of your children. Think about it. They have no control over their lives. None whatsoever. Can you imagine how frightening that must be? During the divorce process your children are treading water in the pool of your emotions. If you don't want them to drown, you are going to have to toss them a life ring comprised of your wisdom and experience to guide them through the adjustment period and beyond. Without your clear knowledge and persistent support, they will become the unfortunate victims of a dysfunctional, splintered family unit. You simply cannot allow that to occur. They are not only the future of this country but they are the ancestors of their children's children. What you do today has a ripple effect for generations to come. Your role in shaping their history cannot be underestimated.

If you're like most parents, at one time or another you have thought, "I don't know how to proceed. Why didn't my child come with a manual?" The fact is, much of life is trial and error. Take marriage, for instance. No one really prepared you for how to live harmoniously with another person twenty-four hours a day for the rest of your life, which is often why we enter into marriage blissfully and end up where you are today. The wedding alone actually divides many couples who have devoted almost a full year to all the preparations and no time to the relationship. Ask most men and they'll agree that once they pop the question and place the ring on her finger, their fiancée goes into planning mode and doesn't come up for air until the big day. Half the time, the bride walking down the aisle is a virtual stranger to the groom, having undergone a complete metamorphosis in order to please all the family members and guests. At this juncture, some couples who are saying "I do" should instead be saying "I don't."

Divorce is another such life juncture which can only be traversed with a crash course in legalities and a whole lot of stamina. Parenting, unfortunately, is also a process of trial and error. For the most part, if we love our children they will forgive us for learning as we go; however, that does not hold true when you are parenting through the divorce process. This is one time when there are no second chances, no margin of forgiveness, no turning the responsibility over to someone else. If you are the biological parent, that will never change as long as you live.

On a positive note, the process of parenting through divorce is one that can be predicted and anticipated. All children experience to one degree or another similar sorrows, hopes, dreams, trust, mistrust, fears and losses. We have written this book to be your manual—the only book you will ever need to fix what is broken and protect what is still whole. These pages will cover vast ground, pointing you in the direction of what you can expect during the divorce process while explaining the consideration your offspring need as they look to you for support. For the purposes of simplicity, we will elect to use one gender, but please be aware that this book is aimed neither at women nor men exclusively. Substitute your own gender where it is applicable, settle back in a quiet room, and allow us to empower you with the confidence of good parenting skills while educating you as you approach confusing times. Let us offer you a new vantage point: what it's like to face family upheaval as viewed through the eyes of your children.

CHAPTER TWO

How Do I Turn in My Title as an Adult?

Ask most children whose parents have undergone divorce and they are likely to recount their position in the family as being directly in the line of fire, lost on a battlefield, assaulted by stray bullets while treading cautiously around land mines. They are subject to everything they hear, and everything they do not hear. They extract statements out of context and try to connect the dots, albeit erroneously, to fit the shattered pieces of their lives back together. Whether you argue with your spouse or maintain a vigil of complete silence, both behaviors are equally hostile and anxiety producing, and both are damaging your children.

We are constantly amazed at the number of people who believe themselves sufficiently clever to code their adult conversations, completely unaware that their children, wearing the hats of little detectives, steadfastly gather clues, measure intonations, skulk around corners, and eavesdrop long after the bedtime lights have been turned off. Their mental notes are carefully stored in the deeper recesses of their minds for later review. Your life is being calculated and scrutinized by minds too young to add up facts and too sensitive to be exposed to adult anger; yet they persevere, not out of curiosity or revenge but out of the need to somehow make sense of what used to be their family, while driven by the mission to somehow repair the damage. Like sponges, they absorb bits and pieces of dialogue, listening even with sleeping ears, and seeing even through closed eyelids. They are weighted down with the burden of despair that has infiltrated the family unit and rattled their security.

There are precious few areas in life in which we have the power to control events; fortunately, determining how we will act to balance our children's environment is one of them.

Whether you consider yourself a detail-oriented individual or you like to fly by the seat of your pants, the divorce process is not the time to leave any detail to chance. Planning is essential, as is reviewing and reevaluating those things that are working and those that are not. For example, you put effort into retaining a seasoned attorney with whom you expect to work as a team to bring to fruition your expectations, you are undoubtedly educating yourself in the arena of family law, you have painstakingly filled out financial paperwork and calculated a dollar amount which you hope to receive in your divorce settlement. Yet, how much effort has been allotted for child rearing? How much of your time will be spent on understanding your children's fears and confusion? You may have assumed that your children will come to you when they have questions or have a desire to express their feelings, but that is not necessarily true, and that is not the norm. Children are reluctant to express themselves. They are afraid of being vulnerable to your answers and they do not want to confront the issues that are tearing the family apart. Also, children rarely have the ability to adequately express their emotions verbally. They simply do not have enough of a grasp on their emotions or sufficient verbalization skills to convey their thoughts, and instead often act out their feelings in dysfunctional ways that cause disruption. Those disruptions are usually met with punishments and time-outs until the children learn to shut down and repress their words, thoughts and actions. Do not underestimate quiet children. They share the same fears, anxieties and anger that aggressive children possess; they simply do not exercise any outlet for those feelings.

Parents often remark that their children are "going through a phase" or "being bad," but these behaviors are the cornerstones of a child's primitive expression. Do not blame your children's defiance and rebellion on "teenage behavior" or "the terrible twos." If you do, you will miss the cues they are laying before your eyes. They are announcing their problems with the divorce or how the divorce is being handled and are asserting that these problems will not fix themselves.

"Good" behavior is every bit as dangerous as its counterpart. These are children who cannot get in touch with their emotions or whose personalities tend to be more guarded, but both are blaming their parents for their inability to find a way to get along with each other and, worse, may be blaming themselves for their imagined part in the spousal breakup.

Here is a wake-up call. While you weren't looking, your children slid past you and are now perched precariously on the back burner. You notice them, but you're not really seeing them because they are masking their emotions and disguising their anger, proficient chameleons at keeping you from their intimate thoughts and feelings while they are suffering the effects of a broken heart and lots of hidden tears. If the child never adequately bonded with one of the parents, it may be easy to overlook their grief, but please be aware that, regardless, the child is deeply mourning the loss of that parent and the opportunity to ever bond with him if he is removed from the house.

Parental loss is not a superficial loss. It isn't a problem that will be all better with a band-aid and a kiss. This is a profound sorrow that makes a child feel sick, that adds words such as "unbearable hurt" and "depression" to their vocabulary.

Children can and do suffer from depression. We must encourage and allow them to talk about their feelings as best they are able, and encourage conversation that offers them opportunity to express their anger and confusion without repercussions. Regardless of your own uncertainty, you have an obligation to assure them that you are in control and have appropriately planned for the outcome of this tumultuous event. You must make yourself believable even in your terror and remove yourself from the spotlight, lest your children have to wait in the wings for their curtain call. If you insist on making the divorce all about you and your concerns, what they will wonder is, "If my parents don't know what they are doing, how on earth will they be able to look after me?"

If your children's view seems self-centered, it is for good reason. Children are by definition self-absorbed little people who do not appreciate their world being turned upside down. You may think they should understand and empathize with your stress and try to accommodate your needs by being more helpful or less demanding, but you might as well save your breath. They are not equipped to deal with your problems, nor should they be expected to. They do not want to be inconvenienced with the notion that their parents cannot get along with each other. You might as well put the responsibility in its proper perspective. They didn't have anything to do with your marriage and they don't want to have anything to do with your divorce.

Parents often place their offspring in the unhealthy position of having inappropriate information confided to them, both as a venting outlet for the parent and to manipulate their loyalties. This is a big no-no. To place your child on an equal emotional level by confiding intimate information that is not age appropriate is to contaminate their childhood. That is nothing if not self-serving, and to try to manipulate them under the guise of conveying information is a cheap shot which has long-term consequences both for the children and for you. This is not their battle. You do not have the right to violate their childhood. While your world may have come crashing down around you, they do not expect that their world will do the same. Unless they have been neglected or abused, and by that we mean in the legal sense, not just in your opinion, they pretty much want their corner of the world to remain just as it has always been. Any attempt by you or anyone else to make changes will be met with anger and resistance.

Children are not stupid and they are not big fans of change. Your attempts to paint a pretty picture of future downsizing or change of housing with the promise of new friendships and new classmates is simply not going to work. The fact of the matter is that you may be forced to move and downsize, but this will be met with disdain, not enthusiasm and support. If you expect anything other than contempt, you have been living with your rose-colored glasses on for too long. Take them off and throw them away. This is going to be an emotionally bumpy road which is going to force you to dig deep in order to be patient and supportive.

Other rose-colored issues involve words like "budget" and "money problems." Don't expect sympathy from your offspring if you are having difficulty paying the bills or working two jobs. They simply don't care, not because they don't love you but because children are adrift in a sea of "I wants" and cannot understand the concept of budgeting. To the contrary, these seeming little gold diggers continue to try to pile on the guilt of doing without until you either lose your temper or cave in to their demands. In their defense, their demands are not necessarily based solely on greed and selfishness but also on the childish notion that if you love them then you will find a way to get them what they want when they want it.

From an early age, money has the connotation of magical fun. Children see adults produce a piece of paper or shiny coins that are traded in for treats that offer comfort and pleasure. Money magically becomes ice cream cones or cotton candy at the fair and, later, stylish clothes and brand new automobiles. Children also see adults spending more than they make to reward themselves with treasures and expect adults to do the same for them. It is just that simple. There is no surefire way of changing their misconceptions with the exception of the maturation process, and even that is questionable. Suffice it to say that money may mean many things to many people, but money means nothing to your children. Regardless of what they have, they will never have enough and, despite your generosity, they will never put their hand back in their pocket.

Now that we have established that children are basically self-centered creatures with unending requests, here is the dichotomy. These same self-centered children will undoubtedly personalize the divorce to some degree, taking the blame for the demise of the family by attributing their parents' decision to separate directly to their own shortcomings.

It is not enough to offer the pat phrase, "You know you didn't have anything to do with the breakup." They're not buying that. Of course they believe they had something to do with the breakup. Didn't they refuse to take the garbage out? Clean their room? Feed the dog? In their world, this was enough to push the marriage to the brink of disaster, especially since there no doubt was a time when you said something to the effect of, "I can't take this anymore," as we all have at one point or another. It might have been a missed chore or a bedtime struggle. It might have been the chicken pox that ran rampant through every member of the household, but at one time or another your children heard that statement, and they've been saving it in their file folder for just this occasion.

Although your children will have a difficult time believing that they are not powerful enough to ruin your marriage, you may be more likely to convince them if you speak to them with undivided attention. Look into their eyes. Hold their hands. Hug them. Make sure they know you mean it. They had nothing to do with the breakup of your marriage. Remind them that children are not expected to be perfect, or even half perfect, and that you, their own parents, were not perfect children. Give examples. "I remember one time when I was about your age that I made my mom so mad when I didn't do . . .," and so on. This is an exercise that should be repeated often.

We don't want to minimize the importance of your children's effect on your marriage, but it is essential they grasp the important notion that their world, important as it is, cannot possibly deflate your world. Children imagine themselves to be extremely powerful short people, and as such they believe they have somehow inadvertently used their powers to split apart the family. They may also try to corral those same magical powers to put the marriage back together again by rabbit foot wishes and licorice pipe dreams. It is your job to communicate effectively that while wishes are not to be made light of, there are some things that cannot be "wished" back together, and your marriage is one of those things.

While we're on the subject of communication, it might interest you to know that children do not have the ability to differentiate between sarcasm and truth. They are very literal people until well into their teenage years, and although you might say things in jest to which they might laugh along with everyone else, they're only taking your lead to join in the fun. They are not laughing on the inside, especially if they are the brunt of the joke. The point of this is that we, as parents, have all slipped up in our communication, saying things we don't mean, exaggerating to make a point, laughing at other people's mistakes. So statements like "I don't know what I did to deserve a kid like you" will translate into "Mom wishes she didn't have me for a child." Curb your anecdotes and your illustrations.

Unbelievably, some of you might really believe that your child was, in fact, the reason behind the breakup of your marriage. Let's be clear. Your children did not cause this breakup. They simply do not have that kind of power, and to believe that they do is to think on their level. If your child is so rude or unmanageable that your marriage has suffered, then change the behavior of your children, not the direction of the marriage. Please don't say you've tried to do that. The success is in "doing," not in trying. It's in taking charge, not in whining. Be the parent your children need you to be. If you want to get control of your life, begin by taking control of theirs.

Hold on! We can almost hear the outcry of child advocates everywhere. Back off! No one is suggesting that children be bullied or abused. We are simply reminding you that children need structure and boundaries, they need clear guidelines and good role models, they need consistency, respect and love, and they need it from you.

Perhaps in your early years of parenting you doubted the necessity of consistency. Perhaps you wanted to "buddy up" to your child instead of being his parent. It may take some effort to regain the ground lost to that habit, but you can and must elevate yourself into your position as parent—a position that is not on the same level as the one your children are on. Children must know what is expected of them, and what is expected of them should be reasonable according to their maturity level and ability. If you're one of the new-age parents who encourage your children to utter every thought they have, even to the detriment of someone else, if you believe that children should be able to express their displeasure and hostility in any manner they please, and if you believe it is reasonable for children to act out against their parents if they are not instantly gratified, then hang on tight, because you're on the ride of your life, without a seat belt. Society is not going to allow your children to express every thought and feeling they have—not in school, not in the workplace, and not in their interpersonal relationships. If you do not parent your children to become well-adjusted members of society by controlling their impulses, you haven't done your job.

Children are born "pleasers." The innocence that allows them to believe they can fix everything and make everyone happy wanes as they are confronted with the reality that not everyone "plays fair." But early on, in their primitive, pure form, they want to make their parents happy and they believe they can do just that. They seek unconditional approval and crave praise for behaving well, but they will take advantage of a crack in the parental system because it is their built-in nature to test the waters. Though they will never admit to it, when they're disrespectful they expect to be called on it, because they know disrespect is wrong. If you allow them to get away with it or, worse, if you behave disrespectfully yourself, you are sending a very powerful negative message. Don't show your ignorance by disrespecting your children or your spouse. We are supposedly civilized human beings with the ability to censor what words come out of our mouths. Children need to be taught by example, or what we refer to as good role modeling, and they need to be given consequences which are fair and enforced to help remind them how they are expected to behave. Rise above your animal instincts and allow your children to feel proud of you or you're sentencing them to a lifetime of becoming you.

Please don't say you would do a better and more consistent job if only you weren't so tired. We're all tired. The whole world is tired. We have taken on too much work, too many hours, too much responsibility, and too much pressure. You have a responsibility to dig down deep and find more energy, the energy you need to parent your child. Being too tired to parent is like putting a toddler on a highway, closing your eyes, and hoping they get to the other side safely. It just isn't going to happen. The bizarre world of parenting is a wonderful, awful, thankless job which will never come to an end. We know there are days when you feel like you didn't sign up for this but, unfortunately, you must not have read the small print. The rewards come later, and they will come. But not before you pay your dues like the rest of us.

If you find yourself married to a spouse who doesn't have the capacity or desire to understand the needs of children or who is jealous of the time that's taken away from him, then you have married an immature person who will continue to jockey for first place. Marriage is a difficult enough commitment without being married to this selfish, inconsiderate and twisted partner, and your job as a parent has probably been more difficult than most. Nevertheless, if there is a choice to be made, then make it. The child stays.

Remember, if children were able to exercise good judgment and control their impulses with consistency, and discipline themselves accordingly, there would be little need for parental guidance and structure, but that's just not how the game is played. There is a myth that it takes a minimum of eighteen years to raise a child. Quite frankly, we put the number at twenty-three years at a minimum. Until then, your children need you to be an integral part of their lives: hovering, protecting, watching, waiting, worrying, closing in and pulling out. Parents are the real role models, the superheroes, and the spiritual, moral, emotional and financial leaders to which children must aspire. Don't disappoint them by setting the bar too high or too low.

While we appreciate the degree of stress that the divorce process produces for the adults, let's try to imagine it from a child's point of view. Through no fault of their own, the two people they love and trust most in the world are fighting. To make it worse, they are refusing to make up. The child has no ability to remove himself from the stress-filled environment that has now become home. Unlike their parents, children cannot call a friend to vent, go for a long ride in the car to cool off, or take in a movie for escape. Their position in the family is one of dependency and helplessness. They cannot call the shots, make decisions, right the wrongs, or even control their own bedtime. They are at the mercy of their parents to restore harmony to the house, or they must live in the chaos. Their pressures are equally as important as your own. They have to worry about being chosen for the baseball team, getting the courage to find a date for the school dance, waking up with pimples, and losing homework. Only you can ease the situation and only you know if you have shirked this responsibility. We are not asking for confession. If you could have done better, it's not too late, but you might be left with quite a mess. Clean it up.

Simply stated, you are the adults, they are the children. The roles are not interchangeable. As adults you should be able to pick and choose your battles. Remember to keep your expectations age appropriate. Children are often impulsive and rude; teenagers need to exert their independence. You do not have rotten kids, but they may be going through a rotten stage. That, coupled with divorce overload, can seem overwhelming, but stay focused, calm and consistent. Remember, what goes up must come down. Don't say things you are going to regret. We all store our life memories in mental filing cabinets, and your children are no exception. Apologizing for words spoken harshly does not eradicate them. Words spoken are words turned loose forever. They are powerful weapons which, if used in a negative fashion, rarely miss their target, inflicting wounds which eventually scar over but never really heal.

That includes conversations between you and your spouse. Your children are venturing close to the battlefield and there is shrapnel flying about. You must protect them from hearing or seeing things that will cause them emotional pain, even if that pain is secondhand. Translation: If you are sad, your child will feel your emotional pain. Children simply cannot barricade themselves against the hostility of an argument. They are both afraid to listen and eager to hear at the same time, piling pillows atop their heads to block out the screaming while straining to hear every last word of the fight. Children are naturally curious, as well as omnipotent in their belief that they can fix anything. They cannot bear your sadness and are willing to carry your burden for you until they come up with a magical solution to make everything all better. Worse, in situations where there may be physical altercations, your children will stay awake all night if need be in order to protect you.

Because children are sleuthing about in the world of mysterious parental arguments, it is inappropriate to raise your voice or make hostile or threatening remarks to your spouse anywhere in the vicinity of your children. You don't understand this. You think that as long as you're not involved in a screaming match your youngster is too absorbed in television to pay attention to the content of your strained voices. Think again. They may be oblivious when they're called in for dinner, but they hear every word that is spoken through two feet of drywall in the dead of night. They also happen to be experts at decoding sentences, even without a Captain Marvel decoder ring. That is just the nature of the beast. So where should you fight? Let us make it simple. Not anywhere inside the house—and not anywhere outside so long as your children are present.

If you and your spouse do not have the ability to control your words and decibel level, know this: Children do not have the capacity to understand disorderly adults. They are not only baffled by the intensity with which their parents fight, but frightened by the extent that one spouse will go in order to hurt the other. You frighten your children when you are out of control. Your children are staying awake nights in order to protect one parent from the other. Imagine the absurdity of that statement. A child of two or three years of age, not yet old enough to pour his own cereal, will lie awake tonight to keep you safe.

So you don't have physical fights? Good for you. How about verbal fighting, or downright slandering the other parent? Talking badly about a parent elicits anxiety on another level. It forces children either to believe the bad information and formulate negative thoughts about the parent in question, or to disbelieve the information and rebel against the accusing parent. Very young children cannot formulate their own decisions and will take your statements as truths, incorporating them as their own. Older children may want to rescue the victimized parent, either aligning themselves with them, or rebelling against you. Even if what you have to say has merit, the more you ask your children to digest the negative statements made against the other parent, the further off course they will veer.

It takes two people to make an argument: the aggressor and the reactor. Don't be either.

CHAPTER THREE

Divorce is Some Nasty Business

There are as many reasons for divorce as there are divorces, ranging from finances to adultery, and none of them is the business of your child. Yet many children still in elementary school can recite line and verse of who did what to whom. How did they get this information? We've already covered eavesdropping, which is not to be minimized, but larger on the horizon looms the real answer. They were told the information by one or both of their parents. What?! Why on earth would you do that? The standard answer, by which we are always insulted, is that you expect us to believe that your child asked direct questions "to which I could not tell a lie." Really? That's pretty funny, because many of the allegations listed in the divorce papers you served upon each other are embellishments of the truth or downright lies. If you think not, reread your divorce papers and you'll know what we're talking about. Sure, your attorney put the allegations into legalese, but if you read and signed the documents, then the inferences and embellishments, which we'll call lies, belong to you.

Even if what you have to say is the truth, how could it possibly be helpful for a child to believe that his mother is an adulteress or his father gambled away the family money? What is the point in telling your offspring that things haven't been going well in the bedroom lately and sex got kind of "boring"? Do you really hate your spouse so much that you've lost control of your ability to censor what comes out of your own mouth? For the most part, your spouse is pretty much the same person they were when you married them, but maybe being irresponsible or blowing money doesn't seem so funny after ten or twenty years, or maybe one of you has grown up and the other hasn't, or you've grown in different directions. There are always reasons to harbor anger. If your spouse cheated on you, for example, you have a right to feel betrayed. What worse betrayal could there be to your self-esteem? But affairs and other indiscretions are merely symptoms of an eroded marital foundation, and that didn't happen overnight or without your knowledge.

If your children do ask questions, be honest without spewing out details. It is perfectly all right to say that you and your spouse don't agree on much anymore and neither of you want the arguing. Or tell them that one or both of you simply hasn't been happy, but remind them that parents can divorce each other without divorcing the children. If you allow your anger and lack of impulse control to get the better of you and you say things you wish you hadn't, go back and repair the damage. If you muddy the waters, your children will have to swim in filth.

There is something known as "alienation of a parent" which we will discuss in detail in an upcoming chapter, but suffice it to say here, your child needs two parents. You might not be a big fan of your spouse, but your children are, and you need to make sure it stays that way. If your goal is to protect your children because you believe your spouse to be an irresponsible oaf who won't keep his promise to pick them up after they've made plans for the day, let the day play out. You may be correct, and if so you can deal with each situation after the fact, not before. Remember, just because your spouse never kept his promises to you doesn't mean he won't keep them to his children.

Perhaps, however, it is your intention to make your spouse look bad in the eyes of your friends and family, and in a convoluted manner you want to deflect attention from your bad traits by illuminating his. Perhaps you feel a pang of jealousy that you seem to have taken on the brunt of the responsibility for the children, while he seems to be having all the fun with them. Worry not. It's the nature of children to choose fun and games over cleaning their rooms, but on some level they realize what's going on, and he won't end up with more points than you. Stability beats inconsistency every time. Making him look bad just makes you look bad, and no matter how much you might want to level the playing field, it's just not worth it.

We're all doing the best we can. Some of us are just better equipped to deal with life than others. Not blurting out every thought we have is a sign of adulthood. Some food for thought: One of the defining moments of adulthood is coming to the realization that even our own idealized or overly criticized parents were just doing the best they could—or not, but stumbling through just the same, as we all are, falling down and finding the strength to get back up. This moment of recognition will come all by itself when the mind is ready to accept what it already innately knows. The next time your spouse stumbles, offer him a hand. He may do the same for you some day.

Deadwood and Other Flotation Devices

Marriages end long before divorce occurs. There is a defining moment between falling in love and falling out of love that is so powerful it can no longer be ignored, but that moment is often denied for years. People cling to deadwood because the fear of isolation and loneliness is more frightening than the fear of staying married to the wrong partner.

People pretend to be in love more than they actually are in love. That is unfortunate for both partners. Worse, many partners continue the public charade, parading about as a happily married couple when their words say one thing but their actions another. When they announce an impending divorce, everyone wants to know what happened. Often, so do you.

So many things can go wrong in a marriage. Mostly, life just happens. Burdens seem heavier, responsibilities become unbearable, dreams are misplaced, and feelings are minimized. Some people seek comfort outside the confines of the marital union, hoping for validation of the person they once were.

Affairs of the heart are often worse than affairs of the flesh. Once emotional loyalty has been broken, it is difficult if not impossible to regain the innocence of what was lost. Intimacies are no longer protected by the sacred covenant of spousal confidence. Character assassinations begin. Deceit starts to weave its layers, one upon another, until the truth is buried. Taking confidences from a marriage and tossing them care- lessly around is more of a betrayal than physical infidelity. It strangles the very core of your existence as a married couple. Sex is sex. It is a huge betrayal, an immoral, cowardly event, and a cheapening of what you as a couple hold dear, but it can never match the power of an emotional affair.

In many ways, marriage defines who we are; it's a public endorsement that we are good enough to be desired and loved. It's the illusion of marriage that we cling to like deadwood riding with the river current, rather than the actual institution of marriage, which by definition implies that two people chose to come together and remain that way, eternally linked by love. Instead, we get tangled in the strands of what was once a warm blanket on a cold night, now just threads unraveling.

Statistically, the odds for a long-term happy marriage are dismal, yet in the human spirit there is a certain optimism that continues to try. Unfortunately, many of us sabotage our marriages and doom them to failure when we romanticize unreasonably our expectations that our spouse will be all things to us, as we will be to them. We believe that if someone loves us they should be blind to our flaws and see us without fault, placing us at dizzying heights. As with everything, when there is nowhere else to climb, the only path is down.

No one person can be expected to meet all your needs, read your mind, rescue you when you want to be rescued, and let you fall if you want to fall. No one person can be expected to earn all the money, do all the chores, exert boundless energy, engage in continually interesting conversation, and be new and exciting in the bedroom every night. Life happens. People get tired or sick, or just sick and tired. There are disappointments and unexpected difficulties. Jobs change, lifestyles are difficult to maintain, dreams fade. People just bail out.

If there were no children to hurt, no little minds to confuse, then divorce might work just fine for most folks. Many people are happy to pick up their marbles and leave the game. But there are children, and they do matter. It is our view that parents should not stay together for the sake of the children if that marriage is filled with arguing and hurling of emotional daggers. But there are marriages based upon reasonable expectations where people just lost their way and need a hand getting back on the path. Those are the marriages that can be salvaged, providing there are equal amounts of love and forgiveness. Those are the marriages that should be resuscitated in marriage counseling.

Divorce is a word tossed around so casually that it has lost its meaning. It is said in anger and in jest to back up threats and issue ultimatums. We need to reacquaint ourselves with the exact meaning of what it is to be divorced. It is a separation, forever permanent, a splitting of an emotional savings account, a severing of a bond in which two individuals promised their undying love until death. Don't use it in a sentence unless you are prepared to back up your statements.

But if you have made up your mind to divorce your spouse, then get on with it. Educate yourselves. Buy some legal advice. Weigh the pros and cons and make a plan. Then, if the marriage cannot be repaired, if you can no longer love your partner, if you cannot obey the marital contract, get out. It is the only fair thing for both of you. But don't leave without treating each other with the care and respect you both deserve.

If you're looking to rack up enormous legal costs, let your attorney be your mouthpiece, cut your communication, and go for the jugular. However, there is another way, a civilized method by which to leave your marital commitments while still remaining kind to each other for the sake of the children. You are in control of everything you do and say unless and until you relinquish that control to another. Please take into consideration that you and your spouse are going to be attached at the hip through your children's academic years, illnesses, accidents, weddings, births and other celebrations of life and death. You might as well also know that for each of you there are many possible partners and that both of you, difficult as it may be to believe, will probably find yourselves with someone else within the next two years. The next person may not exhibit your spouse's irritating traits, but we can assure you they will come with a full suitcase of their own.

CHAPTER FIVE

🌀 Respect, Discipline and Other Archaic Concepts

Once divorce occurs, your family may no longer be together but it also cannot afford to be further split apart. Both you and your ex-spouse are going to have to find some method of communicating with each other civilly and courteously or reap the consequences—and there will be consequences. In order to communicate, you first must have a grasp on impulse control. Taking cheap shots at every opportunity sets the stage for counter-attacks. It's certainly not a secret that people, if cornered, will come out fighting, closing the gates to communication.

Tomorrow is too late to pick up the pieces of your children's lives. This is the day, right now, to vow to put your personal needs secondary to those of your children. This is not up for negotiation. No one is disputing that it's difficult to be friendly toward a spouse who has hurt and betrayed you, but you're just going to have to muster up strength from wherever you can find it, take a deep breath, and take one for the team.

We are living in different times, and life isn't always fair. It wasn't so long ago that finishing your education guaranteed a high-paying job opportunity where you would continue to be successfully employed until your retirement and the presentation of a gold watch as a measure of your value. Those days are over. Nothing is guaranteed, and nothing should be taken for granted.

Both women and men have experienced many changes in regard to gender roles, equal rights, independence, and the like. Women asked for equal pay for equal jobs and now may be rethinking what they wished for, with both sexes overwhelmed by societal changes and pressures. Employment is no longer based on wisdom and experience, but rather on cheap labor and other inequities. College graduates with huge student loans are circling the classifieds without landing jobs. The majority of households have two working parents just to make ends meet, and the financial pressures are enormous. It's no wonder we cannot devote the time we need to nourishing our relationships with each other and our children.

Instant gratification has run rampant in our society, with excesses of automobiles, computers, cell phones, I-Pods, boats, clothing and jewelry becoming the norm. We have become a disposable society, easily discarding what we believe to be outdated, including electronics, vehicles, houses and spouses. We are on stimulation overload, with video games, computer chat rooms, interactive television, and casinos all vying for our attention. Even newborn babies are being assaulted in all five senses with loud bells and whistles that flash and spin in a dizzying fashion. Children are bored before they reach their second year of life. They crave excitement, demand to be entertained with new and innovative machinery.

We are losing our children and we are losing ourselves. Buried beneath day planners and credit card debt, we continue to schedule more, spend more, want more. We search for happiness in bars and shopping malls, movie theaters and poker rooms, and if a partner wants to take a breather from this hyperactivity, we trade them in like a worn pair of shoes. We are a nation marching to the beat of impulse overdrive. Family traditions are being buried with our elderly population. Grandparents, once proudly included and involved in their families' lives, are now fending for themselves financially and physically while their adult children move on without them. Virtual strangers are gracing our holiday tables as "sit-in" relatives, while our own relatives are dining alone.

The floodgates have opened and our children are pouring into society unchecked. If we're too busy to notice that something has gone terribly wrong, we only have to ask them. They feel the instability, even without a barometer with which to measure normal family life, and they medicate themselves with drinking, drugging, and preadolescent sexual activity, taking all the wrong roads. We must regain control of our children and bring them back into a loving family unit, even if that unit is splintered. Divorce is not an automatic permission slip to let our children fall through the cracks, but ineffective parenting is a sure guarantee that they will. You and your spouse will have to put aside your differences, your arguments, your financial battles, and your mudslinging to bring your children back home.

Our children are angry and rebellious, and they are entitled to be. They are confused and disillusioned. Mostly they're trying to find their way in dark, uncharted territory. Children are growing up too fast, exposed to inappropriate attitudes, events and belief systems because their parents are too busy with their own narcissism to notice. They are being fed propaganda from television and newspapers, introduced to dark-side ideas and material via the Internet, inundated with reports of trauma and crime until they have become immune to human suffering. Systems which have been put in place to protect our children from abuse have been backfiring, with children threatening to call the authorities if they do not get their way.

Children need consistent expectations and discipline that molds them into responsible adults, but there doesn't seem to be anyone home to enforce the discipline even if it is expected. Folks, we have a huge problem on our hands, but we can reverse what is happening. We can reclaim our parental respect and duties, but we can't do it single-handedly. One parent is not enough. Raising healthy, functioning offspring takes the guidance of two parents united in the belief that children must be taught by good role modeling.

Unfortunately, there is a stampede of parents searching for cover, afraid to discipline or disappoint their children, afraid to lose their love and affection. This is nonsense. If your children are running amuck, your neighbors' children are running amuck, and our cities' children are running amuck, we as a civilized nation will not survive. There are simply some rules that are not negotiable, but they cannot be instilled by parents who can't control their own anger or impulses in their own households. If you want to get a divorce, go ahead, but don't throw the baby out with the bath water. If you and your spouse can't agree on much, at least agree on this: Together you will have to come up with a game plan—a provision for discipline, a timetable of events, and constructive consequences that your children will not be able to use to divide your united front.

You are perfectly capable of enforcing rules when it comes to your children running in the street, stealing toys from their friends, pulling the dog's ears, or hitting their new baby sister, but you seem ineffective when other rules must be issued and obeyed. The rules are quite simple. First and foremost, there should never be any disrespect of adults, and that begins with parents. If children are spoken to, they are to make eye contact and give straight answers to your questions. Your household is not a dictatorship, but neither is it a democracy. Your child does not make the rules or decide his consequences. He does not get to choose his menu or take stabs at your culinary talents. He does not decide on his bedtime or his chores. If he has an opinion about something, he may certainly express it, but if his opinion is vetoed, he is to do what he is told. Disrespect can also be shown through body language as well as verbally: stamping feet, rolling eyes, staring through you rather than looking at you. Your child knows very well what he is doing, and he can't believe you're allowing him to get away with his sullen attitude or brazenness.

A child should be instructed only once; for example, "Please take out the garbage in the next two hours." If that request is met with resistance, verbal back talk, or a promise that goes unfulfilled, there is a consequence. The consequence should be agreed upon by Mom and Dad prior to incidents and should be upheld at both households. No two parents agree on every method of discipline and every infraction, but if you cannot come to a compromise, seek therapy so both of you feel that you have been directed fairly, and then agree to the commitments you make in the counseling office. Duplicated charts posted at both households are helpful reminders of what is expected of children and what the consequences will be in the event they do not make proper choices.

We are proponents of regular communication between spouses on the issue of behavior and discipline. That doesn't mean a session of bellyaching over how badly the kids are behaving and how tough you have it. Kids are kids. They misbehave. Do not personalize their behavior. Educate them. Keeping the lines of communication open assists both parents in treating the children with respect. Nothing is more of a dead-end communication than one parent upstaging the other with regard to how the children behave at their house. If your children behave well at your house and rudely at your ex-spouse's, it is your job to lend a hand with discipline without comment on the ineffectiveness of your ex-spouse's parenting skills. If you know your children are behaving disrespectfully in any location, it is cause to circle the wagons.

What about lying? That's another nonnegotiable rule. There is no lying. And by the way, while you're trying to enforce this rule, please remember to set a good example yourself. Do not ask your children not to tell Mom that they didn't really serve time-out or that Dad had a date but doesn't want the former spouse to know. This is teaching your children to lie. Also, if your spouse calls to speak with the child, do not tell them that he's already asleep if he's standing right there. That statement now becomes your child's lie as well as yours. And let's not forget the lies of omission: failure to communicate information your ex-spouse has a need or right to know, inferring that "what your Dad doesn't know won't hurt him."

What else is nonnegotiable? Stealing, physical assault, emotional blackmail, abuse of people or animals, and criminal activity are not tolerated. School attendance, speaking when spoken to, and basic civilized behavior are expected. Take a good look at the list. Make sure you and your ex-spouse agree with these nonnegotiable items, practice what you preach, and put them into effect. What are negotiable items? Things like bedtimes, attendance at special events, exceptions to homework such as illness or travel plans, choices of friendships or school activities, piano lessons or joining the swim team. The list goes on and on, but remember, even the negotiable items become nonnegotiable if you make that a rule. Example: If you and your ex-spouse agree that your son can join the baseball team and you've explained to him that baseball is a team effort and it's important that everyone on the team participates responsibly, then you make finishing out the baseball season a nonnegotiable and your child doesn't get to decide he wants to quit. However, that shouldn't mean that after baseball season is over he must rejoin the following season. If you and your spouse agree to this rule, there will be no parental splitting, no division of unity, and no manipulation by your child.

Suppose that in your house there is a rule that your child's room must be cleaned every day, and in Dad's house it must be cleaned once a week. That decision falls into a category of personal preference. Your child will simply have to understand that not everything is done the same way in every household, and some things have more importance in one house than in another. This is not a reason to fight. You and your ex-spouse can agree to disagree on these line items and it will have little or no effect on the long-term emotional well-being of your child. What will matter is the way in which the situation is handled. For example, to say, "It just seems ridiculous that you have to get up fifteen minutes early to make your bed before school when you already get up at the crack of dawn," is both reckless and instigating. A better way to handle this would be to say, "I know you don't like to get up early, but your dad likes the house neat and clean before he goes to work, and in Dad's house that's important. I think you can do it."

By now you might have noticed that approach is half the battle, with maturity being the other half. The mature approach is to identify the problem, decide on a solution, and bring it to resolution. It is just that simple. Three little steps, and yet it seems to defy comprehension. We appreciate that you might not like your former spouse very much right now, that your emotions are volatile and your nerves have been rubbed raw, but that does not excuse anyone from ignoring the importance of problem solving. This manual will guide you to make choices that will promote the emotional health of your offspring while you retain your dignity and sanity. Pay attention.

CHAPTER SIX

Do You Know Where Your Children Are?

Although we don't mean to put the cart before the horse, we have to back up for a moment to talk about the objectives and philosophies involved in parenting. No two people are alike, each bringing into a marriage different beliefs and goals based upon experiences in their own childhood, either positive or negative. Although this certainly would have been helpful to know during your marriage, it is essential to remember as you walk side by side during your divorce.

Looking back on our own parents' expectations and rules, we can see that in many ways we have become our parents. Though we may feel we differ from them in important ways, our familial input still blankets us with memories which cannot be erased. Your spouse brings his family's expectations and their belief system into the marital arena as well. In addition, you and your spouse are unique individuals, with your own thoughts and ideas which you bring into the mix. Consequently, we have quite an assortment of values and beliefs that somehow need to be integrated and honored.

Fighting spouses rarely see the wisdom or benefit of the other's philosophy, preferring to impede anything that is contrary to their own beliefs and values. That is a problem which we are simply going to have to solve by requesting that all child-adults go to their rooms and only mature adults remain.

Important decisions are based on safety, education, health, finances and the display of love and affection. Less important are decisions based on hobbies, sports, playmates, sleepovers and dinner menus. Safety first. If your spouse or ex-spouse encourages your children to participate in activities that are age inappropriate or dangerous, you as a parent have a right to object. However, if your spouse believes that little girls should take dance classes for grace and poise and you believe it's a waste of money, as long as there is enough money in the till, don't be a spoilsport. Dangerous activities might include scuba diving, skydiving, hydroplaning, mountain climbing, crocodile hunting, bear hunting, target practice, and the like. This is not to say that these activities cannot be safely practiced with proper training and supervision, just that most parents would agree that they hold a higher degree of danger.

But what about other disciplines that aren't hobbies or sports? What about manners, for instance? Suppose one parent's family was a stickler for no elbows on the table, while the other's family had relaxed dinnertime rules. This is not a time for power plays. Pick and choose your battles. No one is going to go down the road of ruin and despair because a part of their anatomy touches the dinner table, so try to be somewhat flexible and keep your requests of the other parent reasonable.

There are gender-based differences in child rearing. Some parents expect one behavior from boys and another from girls. Some people parent differently because of their own genders. Let us put in the disclaimer now. None of the following statements is intended to be biased or sexually exclusive, just generalized as we see it. Just as you are entitled to your opinion, we have ours, and here it is: Women are more protective of their offspring than males are. That doesn't mean we don't appreciate the sensitive, cautious male or that we're minimizing the objectivity of women, it just is what it is.

Men tend to be more adventurous and greater risk takers and expect that most things will work out just fine. Women, on the other hand, are generally more cautious, think ahead to possible calamities, and feel anxious when their children stray too far from their apron strings. Neither is right or wrong. If a father takes his son deep-sea fishing, the mother should not jump to the conclusion that he is being careless or irresponsible. In marriage men and women balance each other out; in divorce you are just going to have to work toward compromise to develop confidence, strength, sensitivity and compassion in your children without negative commentary. Statements like, "You're turning him into a pansy," not only have little value, they scream the insecurities of the parent making the accusation. Are you afraid your son is effeminate? Were you as a child called effeminate? Every statement has relevance not only in relation to the current situation but to deeper, more complicated issues which you might want to think about rather than react to automatically.

Food for thought: Children who are inappropriately supervised or pushed into activities in which they cannot excel or that are inappropriate for their strength or age will develop self-esteem issues and anxiety. The world is supposed to be fun, exciting and safe for a child. If your child does not see his world that way, pull back and find out where the kinks are. Children are not going to "grow into" activities by surviving fear. If your child does not want to be on the swim team or get his brains knocked out in a boxing ring, it is his prerogative to decline. There are some sports, football being one, that really can cause injury to a still-developing body and that may cause future problems. Please don't place your children in jeopardy by allowing them to be involved in such activities unless they are properly supervised, trained, dressed and cared for. We have known parents who scream at their children to "get up" after being kicked in the gut during a soccer game or thrown from a horse. Whether they are on the ground from humiliation or just got the wind knocked out of them, they do not have to "suck it up" just because you want them to. If the game is so important, why don't you suit up and get on the field?

Even in simple day-to-day activities females do not watch over their youngsters in the same manner as males, who generally allow their children to wander a little farther afield than their mother would encourage, but that doesn't mean they don't have a handle on the general location of the child. Still, mothers conjure up all kinds of dark scenarios of impending doom, and, unfortunately, in today's world they may not be far off the mark.

Let's recognize one very gruesome fact. In the twenty-first century our children are no longer safe. The imaginary monsters who once lurked beneath your children's beds are now alive and residing in your neighborhoods. They are not easily recognized unless they have made it onto the list of sexual predators, but it might surprise you to know that the elderly gentleman who lovingly tends his roses next door secretly fantasizes about exposing himself to your youngster, given the opportunity. Pedophiles, or people who prey on children for sexual pleasure, blend easily into society and seem to be multiplying at alarming rates. They come in all shapes and sizes, gender and ethnicity, and wear work clothes, clergy robes, police uniforms, and business suits. They may live down the street or, worse, they may reside in the same house as your child.

These are the cold hard facts. Everyone is suspect. Educating your children cannot be effective without educating your children's parents. The truth about child neglect, abuse and death is indisputable, and we need both you and your spouse or ex-spouse to pay close attention to what we are about to say. Molestation of young children has become an all too frequent occurrence which has lifelong effects. It is not safe to allow your children to walk to school by themselves, or for that matter to walk to a friend's house in the neighborhood. Those days are gone. Children must be instructed not to go into public bathrooms without an accompanying adult. They should never venture into anyone's home without permission, and only if you are sure they will be supervised safely.

Have we mentioned that kids are kids? They are gullible and naïve. They think they know everything. They believe they can take care of themselves in most any situation. They are fearless warriors of all things real and imagined. They are vulnerable to injury and death.

Children do not understand how to determine what is a lie and what is the truth. They believe that if someone seems nice, it means they are nice. Predators often befriend children weeks or months before they molest them, sizing up their likes and dislikes, using information about family members or pets as bargaining tactics to keep the child from telling an adult what has occurred. Candy, lost puppies, lost children are all trumped-up lures to coax your child into their clutches. Until a child has developed a sixth sense of what danger feels like, the words "Never talk to a stranger" or "Never get too close to a person speaking to you from an automobile" are simply not enough to ensure his or her safety.

Knowing where your children are, being sure they are not unsupervised around unknown or suspicious adults or young adults, talking to them about each and every activity that occurred during their day, and monitoring any behavior that is out of keeping with what is normal are essential. Even the most astute child will fall for the "Your Mom's in the hospital and I have to take you to her" speech. If you think they won't, practice different scenarios. You'll be shocked at how they'll reiterate the mantra, "I will never talk to a stranger," and then quickly fall sucker to a man crying because his puppy is lost in the woods.

Chilling news stories about child abductions and murders parade across television screens each night in epic proportions. Postcards and milk cartons featuring abducted children are tossed at your door regularly, to the point where they have lost their shock value. These are the faces of children who have been stolen, who are separated from their parents, and who are in danger. Many of them will never be found. If they escape death, they may wish they hadn't, being subjected to unthinkable sexual torture and crime.

Recently, a program called AMBER Alert was initiated to notify the public about lost children, but even such alerts have become ordinary. We don't stop what we're doing and begin searching for someone's child unless the child belongs to families we know in our own neighborhoods. It is just not enough to tuck your child into bed and say, "Sweet dreams."

If your spouse disagrees with the need for such vigilance with your children, you do have real cause for concern. Good parenting means keeping abreast of opportunities and dangers as they present themselves and making plans accordingly. There are predators hunting out there, and every child is open season. Even yours.

CHAPTER SEVEN

One More for Dinner

Whether you choose mediation or trial, your divorce entails common denominators of the legal system that will occupy quite a bit of your time. Each state varies in its requirements for divorce, ranging from uncontested, relatively rapid divorce after mediation and parenting classes, to a waiting period of one year including legal separation. Some states still require grounds for divorce, while others do not. You will have to check with your particular state agencies, but suffice it to say you will still be bogged down with the details of having your entire married life put on a spreadsheet.

Although in later chapters we will touch the surface of what you can expect in dealing with the legalities of the divorce process, including child custody guidelines and the decision-making procedure used in determining child custody, we are by no means qualified to give legal advice, nor will we. We are simply introducing some of the things that occur during the business aspect of the divorce process to those of you who might be inexperienced and wondering what to expect.

Once again, we cannot overstress the importance of communication, because at its best the ability of you and your spouse to communicate will save you thousands of dollars in legal and trial expenses, as well as months and perhaps years of unnecessary heartache and stress. Believe it or not, it is neither finances nor infidelity that causes the biggest problem in negotiations, but rather communication. To begin at the beginning, the ability to express our thoughts and feelings verbally separates us as human beings from all other species. Communication is fundamental to having our needs met. Even young children understand the importance it plays and the satisfaction it provides when they are heard and understood.

Aside from touch, language is one of the most intimate forms of expression that we as humans are able to share. Words are so important, so universally understood, that a single word such as "love" or "death" or "disappointment" evokes a myriad of emotions in the listener. In the English language, a mere twenty-six letters are so powerful that they possess the ability to change laws, profess love, announce birth and say a heartfelt goodbye. Yet, even with this great gift of communication, many of us choose not to make our thoughts and wishes clear, hoping instead that our partners will instinctively know what we are asking if they love us. This is unfair, unreasonable and unjust.

Why then, if we strive to have our needs met, sometimes going so far as to stray from the marriage into the arms of a stranger whom we hope might understand what we need, don't we simply communicate? The answer is vulnerability. No one wants to bare their soul and become so vulnerable they risk the excruciating pain of rejection. But here's the rub. By not asking for what you need, you will almost certainly not receive it, and the more you don't have your needs met, the shakier the marital ground becomes until the very foundation upon which your relationship was built is scrapped by the demolition team of divorce attorneys. It may be too late in your marriage to open yourself up to give and receive honest communication, but it is not too late in the dynamics of the family unit, meaning your children and former spouse.

You can choose your words wisely and still have your needs met, especially if those needs have now become cohesive parenting and civility. However, don't be surprised at how quickly things fall apart if you take a dig at your ex-spouse, because retaliation is one of those automatic, involuntary responses that are sometimes so vicious and right on target that they can't be anticipated. Words cause irreparable damage to children and adults of all ages. If the assault of words were able to be measured like marks from a paintball gun, the bruises left after a heated exchange would be undeniable proof of its damages.

So which of you will be the more mature, insightful parent and break the cycle of cruelty? Civility is not synonymous with giving up or swallowing pride; it shows a remarkable conviction that above all else your children deserve to have their parents treat each other with respect and kindness. It relieves them of the burden of rescuing you from emotional retaliation and abuse.

Proper communication is very simple, beginning with sticking to one topic at a time. We say this because in the early stages of the divorce process any verbal encounter with your former spouse is likely to conjure up hostility and resentment. The conversation begins with one topic and quickly spirals downhill.

There are two parts to communication, the first involving the ability to speak and the second the ability to listen. Once we get past the resistance and begin speaking, we still have to be heard. Often, years of nagging or hurling insults at each other cause the person on the listening end to tune out or to get defensive and not really hear what is being said. Agree to communicate without underlying motives, stick to the topic, listen to each other, and then take a minute or two to process the information before you initiate a response. Knee-jerk responses are all too common ways of swaying the conversation from positive to negative because you are not really hearing what the other person is saying. Look at them. Do they look angry or sad, worried or dismayed? Look at their body language. Are they guarded or defensive? Are their arms folded in front of their bodies to protect themselves? Think of how you have spoken to each other in the past and remind yourselves not to communicate in that manner ever again.

The fact of the matter is this: If you and your spouse can't communicate well enough to sit down and make decisions for yourselves and your children, then you are inviting a judge to become a member of your household. Set a place at the head of the table, because the judge will now be in charge of all decision making, objectively stepping in to dictate, without emotion, decrees that will forever change the dynamics of your family. If you don't like the idea of a new addition to your family circle, then grow up and compromise with each other until you reach an agreement that you both can live with. Otherwise, pass the potatoes, because the judge has a big appetite.

If you cannot be civil to each other on the telephone or in person, then it's fortunate that you're living in the time of electronic everything. E-mail, for example, is an alternative method of communication which has the added advantage of providing a documented record of who said what to whom and in what manner. E-mail can be downloaded and saved for future reference, assuring that schedules will not be forgotten and that information passed on is clear and concise. Further, it will establish how often each of you communicates and whether one of you might be purposely alienating the other by withholding necessary information. If you choose to communicate via e-mail, remember that if it wasn't written, it wasn't communicated.

Speaking of the written word, this is a good place to point out something that holds true not only in the divorce arena but in all of life. Never put anything in writing that you don't want to see appear publicly. Let us repeat. Anything and everything that you put in writing is up for public scrutiny and may come back to haunt you. Words said in anger, threats made in jest, sarcasm and digs will all surface sooner or later, and they will speak for themselves as to the character of the author.

The bottom line is this: You can decide to talk to each other or you can talk to your attorney, who can talk to your spouse's attorney, who will talk to your spouse, and the whole circle will continue, passing GO and collecting two hundred dollars plus per hour. You do the math.

CHAPTER EIGHT

When Did Childhood Get to Be So Stressful?

We all have jobs to do. Some are fulfilling and entertaining, others are thankless and exhausting, but all of us, in our own way, do jobs that are important to the inner workings of someone or something. Your children go to work every day just like you do but, unlike your job, theirs takes place inside a classroom. Many parents forget how difficult school can be and minimize children's "work" as being easy compared to their own. Take our word for it, your children are not cruising by without struggles. Most of you do the same job every day, with variations on the theme, but for the most part, after you have learned what is expected, it becomes pretty much automatic. Whether you're a school teacher or a surgeon, a priest or a ditch-digger, there are few surprises and little that is new. Your children, on the other hand, are inundated with new material daily. They are required to take in that information and process, comprehend, retain and regurgitate it on demand—on tests and in oral and written reports. Their penmanship must be excellent, the context of the material researched accurate and devoid of plagiarism, and their delivery flawless. They must possess a grasp of the spoken and written word, a comprehension of language skills, reading skills, reasoning skills and math skills. They will be asked to sing, dance, draw, act and debate. They will be expected to become proficient authors, voracious readers and effective orators.

As if this isn't enough, they will also have to develop social skills, deal with peer pressure, experience humiliation, rejection and defeat. They will suffer from the often paralyzing fear of failing and the unimaginable anxiety that comes with test taking. Their performance will be graded each day, without exception. They will be required to attend school when they are tired, worried or ill. They will be given little or no leniency for personal problems, and their performance will be publicly reviewed and exposed four times each year. They will not be protected by confidentiality laws from parents, classmates or educators as they matriculate from one grade to the next. Further, they will be disciplined as the school sees fit for actions that are real or imagined, accurate or inaccurate, until they graduate, at which time their records will follow them through college.

This is a whole lot of pressure. In fact, most of us look back on our school career and all that it entailed and agree we don't know how we made it through. Now add to your children's already overflowing plates a home environment of yelling adults, parents who don't come home, parents who are drunk, parents who are dating, mealtimes in which the children fend for themselves, and homework. Homework has become impossibly demanding, sometimes taking your child hours to complete. Then there are tests to study for, reports to write, experiments to do for science projects. Your child needs you to be focused and present to get him through his life.

If you haven't gotten the picture before, we hope you're getting it now. Your children are racing down the path of emotional burnout if you as adults don't put your needs aside to rescue them.

If you and your former spouse have kept the lines of communication open, maybe Dad could help your child with science and math, if those are his strong suits, and English and history could be Mom's department. Maybe you could even share evenings together in the same house until your child understands the material. Maybe, just maybe, you could learn to appreciate your child's situation and decide to be the adults.

CHAPTER NINE

Child Custody Battles and Other Acts of Deception

Deciding child custody is almost always a miserable mess. Unless together you and your spouse can make that decision, someone else will, because the fact is that your children need a place to live.

The residential custody of children should not but often does represent, among other things, possession. Children are not possessions. They are unique individuals who will be spending only a very few years under your jurisdiction before they embark as adults into the world.

The fight for custody can be brutal, lengthy and costly. There are usually many casualties and no winners. Children may be forced to choose a parent, and in the process will experience tremendous feelings of betrayal, hurt, disloyalty and anger. We are putting our children through the mill for our own self-serving gains, often to avoid society's stigma on a parent, especially a mother, who does not "fight for her children." How will it look, parents wonder, if I allow my children to live with the other parent without a fight? Will it make me look like I don't love them? Like I never wanted them? Will the children themselves think I have abandoned them?

From our perspective, in families with two equally skilled parents there is one with whom the children should live, and you both know who that is. The court system would know who that is as well were it not for the mudslinging and smoke screening that deflect the truth. It is an honorable duty to allow your children to remain in the house with your ex-spouse if you believe in your heart that he or she will establish an open-door policy for you to be with them, and that he or she can provide the better environment with regard to safety, neighborhood, finances, supervision, homework and educational assistance.

The problem is this: Aside from having to admit that your children might be better off with your spouse, children in our society come with a bounty, a price on their heads called child support. The parent with whom the child does not reside often has to pay child support to the residential parent. To most people, that is a big, if not the biggest, consideration. Here's the irony: There is a formula listed in your state's statutes which will determine the amount of child support each child will receive based on their age and the parents' individual incomes. Let's suppose, for example, that you, the mother, are asking for child support for two children, each of whom is entitled to two hundred dollars per month times their age until they are eighteen years of age or graduate from high school, whichever comes first.

If you have a twelve-year-old child and a fourteen-year-old child and you multiply their monthly child support allowance until their eighteenth birthday, you might receive a little more than twenty thousand dollars. Guess what? By the time you've paid both of the attorneys, gone to mediation and paid the mediator, gone to trial without a judgment, undergone a court-ordered custodial evaluation by a forensic psychologist over a period of several months, and then gone back to trial, the tab might well total fifty- to one-hundred thousand dollars. Now, you tell us, where is the logic in that equation?

Still, it's your dime, but let's remember one other important fact. Just because you spent all the money doesn't mean you win the prize. Someone will be the residential custodial parent, and unless there are extenuating circumstances, probably you will share custody, meaning each of you will consult the other before making any major decisions with regard to your children.

In today's complex world, many judges still make rulings from the bench, meaning that after your trial he takes the evidence and testimony and declares then and there who is awarded residential custody. However, more and more judges are calling in forensic psychologists to assist in making that determination. These experts are licensed clinical psychologists who have been further trained in forensic areas as well as in child custody procedures.

The forensic psychologist will engage the family members in an arduous, lengthy and costly set of evaluations and testing in order to make his determination fairly and objectively. After all, the decision he offers the court holds quite a bit of weight and will often determine the course of the children's lives. He will interview every member of the family, both individually and together: the parents, the parents with the children, the children separately and together. He will read volumes of court testimony, depositions, letters and affidavits from family and friends. He will conduct interviews with other family members and review photographs and other personal documents. He will administer tests and evaluate the results. He will then write an in-depth report of your entire life as it pertains to each family member, with his recommendations for custody. The judge will then take the psychologist's recommendation into consideration, usually in conjunction with a trial to allow each attorney to confirm or rebuff the findings. By day's end there may be no decision from the bench, and by year's end there may be continuing additional evidence which further delays the judge's decision. The children, of course, are living with one parent temporarily, and that spouse is usually getting some type of financial assistance from the other.

It shouldn't be hard to comprehend that the psychological evaluation is a good time to put your best foot forward. Often, in order to look better, one parent assassinates the character of the other with obvious ulterior motives. Some spouses even go so far as to make allegations which are untrue and criminal in nature and get the children to conspire with them. A common and quite frankly transparent allegation is child sexual abuse by the father. A child battery allegation, once made, takes on a life of its own, snowballing its way rapidly into the legal system.

We always wonder, how low can you go, really? If there was sexual battery going on, don't you think you might have wanted to call attention to it sooner than when it became convenient as an issue in the divorce? Some unscrupulous attorneys actually have been known to suggest that if there has ever been physical or sexual abuse it would be a guarantee that the abusing parent would be out of the running for custody. Another disclaimer: This is not to suggest that most or even many divorce attorneys are unscrupulous. Most are ethical and law-abiding. We're not even suggesting it was your attorney who gave you the idea. Maybe you have low-life friends. Maybe you have a wicked imagination. Maybe you just watch too much television. In any event, let's take a walk down Allegation Lane and find out where such allegations lead.

First and foremost, any professional—and that includes physicians, psychologists, social workers, teachers, and anyone else with a civic duty or conscience—will immediately report this allegation to the authorities, and it is likely the accused parent will be arrested and taken to jail. When the parent bonds out of jail, he is generally forbidden to see his children until a determination is made as to whether the crime was, in fact, committed. This process involves detectives, depositions, lie detector tests, child endangerment teams and medical doctors, plus physical examination of the child and psychological assessment by a social worker or psychologist. The accused parent will have to hire a criminal defense attorney, who will probably order a psychosexual evaluation of his client, hoping the results will disprove the claim. Meanwhile, the accused parent's employer cannot afford to have a possible felon on the job, especially if that job involves any contact with children, so the accused will probably be suspended or terminated.

With no money coming in from Dad's job, Mom and the kids are having a tough time making ends meet. Mom wants to recant her statements but can't because of perjury charges and possible arrest. The house goes into foreclosure and the money runs out. Oh, and by the way, the child who has lied for Mom has become weary of the game and the story falls apart. By the time Dad is exonerated, there is not much left to fight over.

This is not to say that we don't take a strong stand on any type of child endangerment. We absolutely do. But come on, folks, let's get real. When the trump card doesn't get pulled out until there is a custody battle, it does look suspect. Oh, and here's a thought for you. If Mom knew the child was being abused but didn't make a report to the authorities, she has her own set of legal problems, involving child endangerment by neglect as well as "aiding and abetting." The bottom line is this: Once you begin the web of deception, the person you might catch is yourself.

In legitimate custody fights, judges rely upon outside sources such as forensic psychologists to gather factual information. Collecting that information requires clinical interviews with all parties, including the children. Okay, you might be saying, just ask the children. They should know. Well, yes and no. Unfortunately, children are not always reliable witnesses—reporting what they believe they have seen and heard, rather than what actually happened—nor do they always have an accurate grasp of time and numbers. Something they said happened last night might have occurred six months ago, and a one-time ordeal might be reported as a continual problem. Aside from the accuracy problem looms another which is much worse, and it involves "coaching." We all do it. It's human nature to assist your children in helping you fight for what you believe you're entitled to have. This is not only unfair but it plays emotional games with your children's minds. They don't want to talk badly about either parent, but they don't want to displease anyone either; hence, discrepancies. When children lie, the greater problem is not the manipulation of the events but rather the long-term effects of the anger, confusion, resentment and rebellion the children harbor toward a parent for having been placed in that position.

Your children are not child actors. They may be able to act through a half-hour Christmas pageant, but in real life, faced with months of repeating themselves to detectives and police officers, their stories will eventually begin to deteriorate. Like the obedient little troopers they are, they may have memorized their lines flawlessly, but they have few cognitive resources with which to answer unexpected questions in a manner that is believable. Their body language does not support their accusations; their chronological age does not match up with their spoken and often obviously memorized words. For example, if a four-year-old child says to a forensic psychologist, "My Daddy just keeps on gambling the rent money and I don't know how we'll manage next month," it's reasonable to assume that he has become the mouthpiece for his parent.

Another big no-no is brainwashing, and it still exists, ready and able to corrupt young minds and contaminate their little psyches with inaccurate information based upon your ignorance and greed, with life-long effects. Impressionable children—and they are all impressionable—assimilate information and process it as if it were their own in pretty short order and it rapidly becomes "truth." This is dangerous territory. Your need for more money or a better settlement does not constitute a right to meddle with your children's childhood innocence. If you believe the trauma caused by their lying or feeling betrayed by the other parent will all blow over when they grow up, make sure you put aside some of that money you sold your child's soul to get, because they're going to need it for years of therapy.

Just because you and/or your child have made accusations, true or false, it does not seal the deal. A team of professionals that includes attorneys, judges and psychologists will have to sort through hours of testimony and transcripts—spoken under oath, by the way—and evaluate the merit of the charges based on their evaluation of the relevant facts and the character of the family members involved. Better everyone just tells the truth and let the cards fall where they may. If you have to lie, or coax your children to align themselves with you, you might want to re-examine your motives and your character, because at least one of them seems to be in question.

CHAPTER TEN

Garbage and Heavy Suitcases

So the question becomes, with whom will the children reside? Usually that question is clouded by emotions, and those emotions become the runaway train that eventually derails with casualties. This question is laden with variables which generally support one parent over the other as the most appropriate residential custodian. The courts take into consideration the gender and ages of the children and the care-taking history of the parents: which one has been the more nurturing, supportive, and hands-on. This is not to say that if Dad has been working two jobs to support the family and Mom has been a stay-at-home mother with the time to take the children to doctor and dentist appointments, Dad is automatically counted out. But often there is one parent who makes the time to join the P.T.A., volunteers to make the hot dogs at baseball games, supports school fund-raising, and shows up at every school play. And that counts for quite a bit.

If both parents have been exemplary with regard to their offspring, the decision becomes more difficult and heart-wrenching, even for the professionals. No one wants to see a parent separated from his children, but unfortunately the laws of physics do not allow for one child to exist in two households at the same time. The knee-jerk reaction to child custody is "getting" the children at any cost, but sometimes that cost is great, not only financially but also emotionally. If you are not inclined to serve home-cooked meals on a regular basis, if your strong suit is not patience when it comes to science projects and homework, and if you enjoy a full social calendar, you really should think about allowing your spouse to have residential custody, provided that he can meet most of those needs. Your children will not love you less nor think ill of you if you voluntarily "give them up." In fact, they might compare notes with some of their friends and recognize the emotional turmoil you prevented and be extremely grateful.

But suppose you actually believe that your children are better off residing with you? Does that mean you shouldn't fight for them just because it will be traumatic and costly? Of course not. Just don't fight for the sake of fighting. Look down the road and introduce reality into your realm of conscious thought. Is dating a must on your horizon? If so, where does that leave your children? Alone, that's where. Because regardless of how fabulous the new person is, your children will have some degree of contempt for them out of loyalty to the other parent.

This might be a good opportunity to interject another consideration. Many of you who have decided to leave your spouse have someone else waiting in the wings. Statistics support that the "someone else" who thought you were terrific when you had covert meetings or exchanged electrically charged glances across a crowded room will not be quite as smitten when you're at home wiping up the remnants of your child's stomach virus or dealing with his temper tantrums. The message is this: Don't leave Mr. Wrong for someone who has not seen you through the worst of times. Parenting is just that. Parenting. If it was supposed to be something else, it would be called dating. Your children will be grown soon enough and there will be plenty of time for you to rediscover your identity as a human being minus the kids, but if you don't have someone in mind, don't go looking. Take time and spend it with your children. The memories you make together will be priceless.

If you have other concerns, however, about the ability of your soon-to-be ex-spouse and his parenting skills, you must fight to keep your children in a safe, loving environment, and if that is with you, then so be it. But this is a time to be honest. If it's about the money, about the child support, about what your friends and family will say, then it's about time to grow up. Make your decision to fight for residential custody or not based on the needs of your children and not on your own. Ask yourself this question: If I didn't get one dime of child support, would I still fight for the children? If the answer is unequivocally yes, then fight for them, but remember your resolution with regard to the money. Don't go after more than you should, because anything you get is more than you were ready to settle for. Remember, what you want is the kids.

Children are often used for purposes of retaliation when one spouse has hurt the other, such as is the case with infidelity. Don't make them fight your battles. Maybe you should wave the white flag and call a truce. You do not have the right to inflict pain on anyone. Stop trying to control everything and everyone. Focus on what's important. Provide a stable, loving environment so your children can be children for as long as possible. They don't need to know or understand how the adult world works yet. Their childhood is supposed to look and smell good; it's supposed to be clean and pure. Don't expect your children to empty your personal garbage cans.

Some of you might say at this point, "Well, no one ever protected me from any hurt," or "Well, I didn't have such a great childhood and I turned out okay." Our answer to that is, "No, you didn't." If you didn't have a good childhood, the emotional suitcase that accompanied you into adulthood is filled with stuff that needs to be resolved. Instead of wasting your energy dating, why not give yourself the gift of finding you, learning who you are, unearthing what you lost, and liking who you have become? Because you didn't get a break as a child doesn't mean you shouldn't give your children one. They haven't done anything to deserve fighting, divorcing parents, and they surely don't deserve anything that even remotely resembles brainwashing, coercion, deceit or guilt. Clean out your suitcases. They're weighing you down.

Again, if after all this you and your spouse cannot make the decision of residential custody without a third party, that is exactly what you will get. But be prepared. Nothing that has been part of you will be hidden, and everything you have ever said and done is about to be publicly scrutinized, skewed in such a way that even you might not recognize your own life.

Attorneys are great investigators and debaters. They are magicians and storytellers. Each of you will have something less than desirable to say about the other, and some of these statements can be supported by past employers or lovers, neighbors or estranged family members. These people will surface like stains on fabric, ready to put in their two cents with their inaccurate recollections and biased information. Nothing is quite as juicy as a nasty divorce.

Everyone has something in their past they are not proud of, but if your past has become your present, if your behavior is tainted with blemishes, you might want to bow out gracefully before your untimely demise. If you have, for example, a craving for drugs or alcohol, if you enjoy giving your children a good beating, or even if you frequent nude beaches, prepare yourself for a lengthy and ugly battle.

CHAPTER ELEVEN

A Good Fight Sometimes Goes Fifteen Rounds

So you've decided to fight. If it's for the right reasons, good for you. Be prepared, however, for a very bumpy ride on a long and winding road. You are about to enter the world of legal documents filled with terminology with which you might not be familiar. Let's begin at the beginning. Without giving legal advice, for which we are not trained, we can caution you about some of the more common situations that occur during the divorce process.

One of the points of interest is this: some lawyers want you to be the one to file for divorce first, the idea being that your partner may be caught off guard. Also, many attorneys feel there is an advantage to being the aggressor. Filing for divorce does not mean that you are getting a divorce. It simply means that you have the desire to get a divorce, to no longer be married, to no longer be joined financially or legally. If you use an attorney to file for divorce, that attorney will likely ask for what is called a "retainer," an amount of money which you must put down, like a down payment, on the services you are about to receive. Some attorneys will give you a set figure for the divorce, but most will be billing at an hourly rate which, depending on your geographic location, could be anywhere from one-hundred to as much as five-hundred dollars per hour.

Billable hours are not just those that are mounting while you're speaking with your attorney but continue to accrue as he makes telephone calls, communicates with your spouse's attorney, reads mail, sends copies of motions, files motions, and engages in any other activity that has to do with your divorce proceedings. You should ask your attorney for a copy of these costs monthly, because if there is a charge that you don't agree with, it's almost impossible to argue with it months later. Your attorney's secretary or paralegal may be billing you as if they are the attorney; in other words, if it takes the paralegal an hour to research a motion or the secretary fifteen minutes to get your paperwork typed for docket call, each one of those hours, or partial hours, will be billed at the attorney rate. In other law firms the secretary or paralegal bills at a lesser rate. It is up to you to ask the important financial questions before you retain an attorney.

Filing for divorce is usually a good thing to do, although many couples take the tack that they can work the agreement out themselves. We doubt that. In our experience, all you're doing is showing your hand, allowing your spouse to know your weaknesses, and making deals without legal expertise. Even if a deal is struck between the two of you, that deal often falls apart when one or the other of you confers with an attorney "just for good luck" before signing. The attorney will offer views on the shortfalls and downsides of the agreements and everyone marches quickly back to square one with hurt feelings, anger and resentment. If both you and your spouse are willing to be fair, then be fair with attorneys at your side. They have a fiduciary and ethical duty to tell you if you are not making the best deal for yourself, but they will honor your decision to be less than ruthless if you are firm.

Spouses who do not want attorneys involved are usually spouses who either don't want to spend the extra money or who have something to hide, or both. Spend the extra money. Remember the old adage, "Penny wise and pound foolish"? In divorce, the amount of money you actually spend to get an agreement right the first time will be less than you spend trying to fix the botched do-it-yourself agreement later. Lay people do not know the wide parameters of the law and make costly mistakes. For example, generally an inheritance or disability settlement is not considered to be part of the marital assets unless the proceeds have been put into a joint asset such as a family homestead, but still those moneys will be awarded wrongly without direction and expertise. Again, your attorney is an extension of you. If you want to be fair and equitable, then that is the deal he will present. If your spouse agrees that it is fair and equitable, then the divorce agreement is executed. It's as simple as that. If your spouse does not want to be fair and equitable, you'll find that out straightaway. No amount of persuasion by your spouse's attorney can turn an honorable person into a dishonorable one. If the deal falls apart, it is your spouse who foiled the plan, and you're better off knowing where the characters in this cast stand early on.

A word about attorneys. They are not your best friend, nor are they your babysitter. Because you are paying them a hefty sum of money, you may feel entitled to their undivided attention, but you will be sadly disillusioned. This is your only divorce. This is not their only case. Generally, attorneys put the gears in motion in stages. Stage one is when they have their initial meeting with you, stage two is when they draw up the allegations that will be filed against your spouse, stage three may or may not be during the mediation process, and stage four is definitely saved for trial. Other than that, there may be weeks or even months when there is nothing going on with the case, time when your attorney is waiting for paperwork to be filed or interrogatories or financial affidavits to be supplied. The divorce process is a game of waiting—a time of patience, frustration, anger and anxiety. Don't take it out on your attorney. If you did your research and chose wisely, then allow him to do his job. He knows what he is doing. No offense, but you don't.

How you choose your attorney is strictly up to you, but two of the best methods are by reputation and word of mouth. If you know someone who was satisfied with their relationship with their attorney, that's a sign that at least the attorney must have paid attention to detail and followed through on promises made. Speaking of promises, do not choose an attorney based on what he thinks he can get you in the divorce. He knows what the law says you're entitled to, and he has experience with cases similar to yours, but he has never negotiated a divorce between you and your spouse, with all your variables and unique eccentricities that cannot be predicted. Therefore, take what you believe you will "get" with a word of caution. The only thing you can count on is that you will know the outcome of the process when the process ends, and not before.

After you have retained your attorney, you might want to put on your running shoes, because you will be doing all the running. There will be information to be obtained and researched, documents to be filled out and researched, financial affidavits to be completed and researched. In other words, you will be doing a lot of research.

If you don't know what your bills are because you do not pay them directly, don't count on your spouse to fill in the blanks. Telephone the electric company, the water company, the cable television company. Inquire with the pest control people, the phone company, and the automobile insurance company. It is your job to have every fact and figure that you can get your hands on, and most of them you can obtain. If privacy acts governing contracts that are in your spouse's name alone prevent your getting the information, your attorney has the ability to subpoena those companies and get what you need. Ask for printouts for the past year, not just estimates, and ask for them in black and white. This is not the time to rely on your memory, because by the end of this process your memory will be filled.

Monitor telephone calls and mail. Look at return addresses for clues to information your spouse may not have made you aware of, such as investing companies or banks in which you do not have a joint account. There are clues all around you, every day, and if you pay attention you'll be amazed at what you will learn. Opening mail that is not addressed to you is not wise, nor is it legal. The same with taping telephone conversations. These are federal offenses and will give you problems you don't need. Also, taping conversations without the express permission of the individual being taped is not only illegal, but the tapes are inadmissible in court.

Why do you need to gather all this information? Because some spouses hide money. Some spouses lie on their financial affidavits. Some spouses are low-down cheating scoundrels with agendas that do not involve honesty and integrity. Don't expect your attorney to be your evidence gatherer, but do expect him to make use of the material you bring forth. If for any reason you don't feel that your attorney is representing you in the manner you expect, you certainly may fire him, but be prepared to walk away without your retainer. Most attorneys do not refund money, nor do they wipe away any bills incurred because you've had a change of heart.

Let's be clear about exactly what filing for divorce means. It means that you are actually suing your partner for divorce. The key word in that sentence is "suing." Once a lawsuit is filed, any and all documents are public record, meaning that your attorney, as well as your spouse's, have the right to any and all evidence which will assist them in representing their clients. Nothing is private. Not money matters, past behavior, present behavior, old and new lovers. Not debts, bankruptcies, substance abuse, physical altercations, mental and physical health records. Not parenting behavior. Information asked for will be information received, and unless you and your spouse have a chummy agreement to keep the dirty laundry hidden, don't be too surprised when he pulls out all the stops.

"Interrogatories" are written questions served by one party's attorney upon the opposing party for the purpose of gathering pre-trial information. Written responses under oath must be provided within a specified period of time. Because this is a legal document, it subjects you to perjury charges if it is not filled out honestly. The questions may be about money, real estate, stocks, bonds, and other property which may be held either jointly or separately. There may be questions about child rearing or infidelities. You may be insulted by the questions and your spouse may be insulted by your answers, but that's what makes the game interesting. Remember, questions reveal the direction in which the opposing attorney may be heading.

Interrogatories complement the financial affidavit, which specifically asks about any and all property, money, jewelry, income and debts that you hold either individually or jointly, or associations or corporations which may be separate from marital holdings. The financial affidavit also includes questions referring to any moneys obtained from disabilities, lawsuits, inheritances, life insurance policies and the like, as well as real estate or tax shelters which may be assets or liabilities.

Speaking of taxes, here's a warning which can save you a lot of grief. Do not sign your name to anything unless you read and understand where your signature is going. We know of a very aggressive attorney who had a very dependent client who came into the divorce process without much information or knowledge about her spouse's holdings. On her financial affidavit the client listed "condominium" under the assets column because she recalled that her spouse had made that investment. In the divorce proceedings, she adamantly insisted on possession of the condominium, along with other assets, and was happy to be given it without reservation. The caveat to this story is that the condominium she was awarded turned out to be a disallowed tax shelter for which the Internal Revenue Service expected to be repaid for income that had not been taxed over a period of many years. Because she now owned the investment, the IRS came to her for the back taxes. Later, after sorting out the costly error, the IRS came to her for half of the back taxes since she had signed the tax statement every April 15th in the joint tax return she filed with her husband. Is the attorney culpable? Well, he's sorry. He's not perfect. The moral of the story is, again, know what you are signing, know what you are asking for, do your homework, and don't take anything for granted. If it looks too good to be true, it usually is.

If you're like many spouses who simply sign the yearly tax papers without inquisition, go back seven years and get copies from your accountant. Bring these copies to your attorney or sit down with a forensic accountant or someone you trust independent of your spouse who has the expertise to interpret these forms for you. If there are mistakes or discrepancies, point them out to your attorney immediately. In the case of the tax shelter and the dependent client, she was eventually absolved of her financial obligations to pay back the taxes owed because the Internal Revenue Service deemed her to be an ignorant spouse, but that verdict took two years and plenty of unnecessary worry. If you are ignorant, get an education. Being deemed an ignorant spouse is nothing to brag about.

Depending on the state in which you live, mediation may or may not be a prerequisite prior to obtaining a court date. The purpose of mediation is to prevent tying up the court system with cases which could otherwise be solved or mediated without a judge. A mediator trained in divorce mediation temporarily replaces the judge in the sense that he can write up marital settlement agreements and help couples achieve their goal of separating assets without a long and costly court battle. Mediation can prove fruitful if the couple is close to an agreement but stuck on a few areas or if a couple agrees in advance that they will abide by the mediator's advice and knowledge about what is a fair and equitable settlement. Mediators are usually paid an hourly rate, with a minimum set number of hours. This fee is generally split between the two spouses and is paid at the time of mediation at the hourly rate set by the mediator, which may be two- or three-hundred dollars per hour. The total bill includes not only time spent during the mediation process, but also the behind-the-scenes work product completed by the mediator and his or her clerical staff, as well as the time spent typing the mediation documents and filing the court paperwork to be presented to the judge at the time of the actual divorce.

If a case does not settle in mediation, the attorneys enter into what may become an arduous process, including deposition taking. What is a deposition? A deposition is testimony taken down under oath in the presence of a court reporter in response to questions by either your attorney or your spouse's attorney or both. You will be asked to answer to the best of your recollection questions ranging from the elementary, such as your name and address, to those which are more complicated, such as where and with whom you spend your Wednesday evenings. If you do not recall, that is your answer. It is an answer which may frustrate the opposing attorney, but his frustrations should not intimidate you into answering questions which may be inaccurate or unfair.

In the deposition process, your demeanor is essential because you are not only expected to be forthcoming with information but you are being assessed as to how you hold up under stressful questioning, whether you can be agitated into losing your temper, and how a judge or jury will evaluate your demeanor in the courtroom. There are many witnesses who have lost cases not because of the information they gave but because of their demeanor and credibility. You may be harassed and exposed in an unfair light. The opposing attorney may lower himself to infer that your reputation is tarnished or your parenting skills are abhorrent. At the end of the day, if you have kept your composure and given information as best you were able honestly and calmly, you've done your job.

During depositions, many opposing attorneys count on the witness—that's you—to volunteer more information than what is being asked. Many witnesses feel they are not being understood or are being presented unfairly and want to clear up misconceptions with defensive ramblings. Don't fall into this trap, and it is a trap. Answer questions asked and nothing more. Do not explain anything. Do not guess at answers. If, for example, an attorney asks how many nights in the past year you have read your child a bedtime story, the appropriate answer is either, "Every night," or "I don't recall." Any other answer will get you into trouble later if you should be redeposed or when you are on trial. Why? Because when you put specific numbers to an event, the attorney will later be able to discredit you if you can't recall the exact number you stated in your original response. So even if you honestly believe that you read your child a story thirty times last year, if you later say forty or twenty, your answer will be used to discredit you. It is best to say "I don't recall" in a deposition and save your exact number for trial.

You may feel extremely anxious prior to your deposition being taken, but take heart. The attorney can't know any more than you tell him, and the only person in the room who really knows what you are about to say is you. That puts you in the driver's seat and him in the backseat. Another reason you might feel anxious is that your spouse will be present. That's true. He has a right to be in the room, and to unnerve you he and his attorney may pass notes back and forth, or he may whisper a comment to his attorney following one of your answers as if to tell him you're a liar. That's fine. No one cares what they do or say. This is not about them, this is about you. Look at this deposition as a time when you and your attorney are also on a fact-finding mission. From the opposing attorney's questions you will get an idea of where he and your spouse are coming from, or what inconsistencies your spouse might have told his attorney that you will later be able to clear up by providing facts.

A last note on deposition taking. The winner of this game is the witness who states the truth in the least amount of words possible, without volunteering one extra syllable. Questions which can be answered with yes or no should be answered exactly that way. Questions which seem to be leading you down a path of bramble bushes and quicksand can be answered with, "I don't know," or "I don't recall." If there is something that has to be cleared up, your attorney will get a chance to cross-question you at the end. If he waives his right to do that, you've done a good job. The biggest favor you can do for yourself is to remember these words: If you have to take a breath in the middle of your sentence, you've said too much.

CHAPTER TWELVE

Check, Please!

There will be times when you feel like giving up. You will be stressed, inundated with paperwork, agitated by a seemingly endless process that feels like a big hole in which you continue to throw money, and you will have little patience left over for the children. Remember, this divorce is necessary for both you and your spouse to begin your lives anew and for you to take inventory of how you got into the position of being married to the wrong person and how you will learn from your experiences.

The divorce process will end at some point, usually within one year unless the state in which you live requires a waiting period. However, we cannot lose sight of what will not end, and that is the impact this divorce and your behavior will ultimately have on your children. Look at children and you will often see the parents. If your children are acting out or seem anxious, they are feeling your stress. If you are behaving in a manner that seems to them to be helpless and overwhelmed, they will begin developing traits of depression or anxiety which may be temporary or become a permanent part of their personality. They may develop an obsessive-compulsive need to keep their world neat and orderly because the environment at home seems so out of order. Your children are the mirror image of what they see in you. For their sake, you are going to have to find within yourself some measure of solace, harmony and forgiveness.

While you are buried beneath paperwork and court documents, you might also be fighting for temporary support from your spouse. These are hard times, but they will pass. In the meantime, try to exercise some logic and good judgment when it comes to your children and your household. For example, if your spouse is supposed to pay the electric bill but hasn't and you have the ability to pay it, do it. Although some attorneys may advise you not to pay it, they won't be the people sitting in the dark without air-conditioning all night or all weekend. Just because you pay a bill that is due when it has been deemed your spouse's responsibility does not mean that a judge won't order your spouse to pay you back later. Do the right thing. Your child is already afraid of the dark. You're not going to win any points by putting him in a pitch-black room and telling him he can thank his Daddy for it. He expects you to fix the problem, and quite frankly so do we. Anything that places your child in danger or creates fear that is in your control to minimize or alleviate you should do, no questions asked.

Do not give up. That's what your spouse and his attorney want. It is what they're waiting for. They think you don't have the stamina for all this, but perhaps they have underestimated you. Perhaps this divorce has made you a stronger person and empowered you with confidence. There is nothing more sweet than not folding under pressure. Take each day by itself. You can master the task, face the challenge, achieve the goal, or at least darn well stay in the boxing ring. All you have to do is wait for the bell to ring and you'll be able to rest in your corner. All you have to do is make it through fifteen rounds and you win, or at the very least you don't lose. Look at the faces of your children and remember what you are fighting for. It's not the money. It's not the marital residence. It's not the boat or the summer cottage. It's the safety and security of the family, because even without everything else, if you have that, you have it all.

Even with your parenting skills scrutinized, even with your spouse fighting over possessions or custody, you can still take a break, still unwind without the children, still be a great parent and not be attached to your children twenty-four hours every day. Get a sitter and have dinner with friends. Get a haircut and a manicure. Go to the library and lose yourself in a good book. Put the kids to bed early. Give them waffles for dinner. One night of no cooking won't hurt. In fact, they'll thank you, and you'll thank you when you wake up refreshed and ready to tackle the next day. Downtime and restful sleep are the best medicine for stress, and we are nothing if not resilient.

No one likes to be under a microscope, but if you're doing nothing wrong and your demeanor is calm and patient, we say let them look all they want. If you give them nothing to take away, they leave empty-handed.

CHAPTER THIRTEEN

Conspiring Minds Want to Know

Another word which carries a lot of weight in custody cases is "alienation." The judge will make his decision about who will make the better custodial parent based upon many criteria, but certainly he wants to ensure that the parent with whom the children do not reside will be encouraged by the residential custodial parent to maintain a loving and nurturing relationship with them. The judge believes, and rightly so, that each parent has something to offer that can benefit the children's growth and development in ways which cannot be underestimated. He understands that if one parent sabotages the children's relationship with the other because of ignorance, immaturity, anger or jealousy, it is likely the children will suffer the consequences of parental estrangement and loss, perhaps for all time. Therefore, it is of great importance that you and your spouse show your ability to communicate with each other with respect. Should one of you stand in the way of communication between the other parent and the children—for example, by making flimsy and transparent excuses about why he or she wasn't given information about the children's school or extracurricular achievements or about illnesses or appointments—that parent will be the one considered to most likely alienate the children from the other parent and will probably not be deemed a good choice as custodial parent.

Here's the amazing thing about sabotage. It works for a while, but it doesn't work for long. Sabotage and alienation are easily identified. If a child is not allowed to receive telephone calls from the nonresidential parent because the child is always "busy" or "resting," regardless of what time of day it is, it becomes obvious that the child is being distanced.

There are also subtle, covert ways of alienating, such as not remembering to tell the other parent the date and time of the school play or that little Johnny's teacher has called a conference, and once the parent has been distanced, the child begins to believe that he is simply not interested or is too busy to attend. The child begins leaving the parent out of the loop as well, so saddened that he has been rejected in the past that he protects himself from future pain.

The bottom line is this: Regardless of whether your spouse wants to attend a meeting, whether or not he has attended meetings in the past, and whether you suspect he will never attend any in the future, you do not have the right to deprive him of the opportunity to be an equal participant in your child's life. If he doesn't show up, will your child be disappointed? Yes. Will your child be hurt or angry? Yes. But that's life, and you cannot interrupt the natural course of your child's life. He has two parents. If one elects to be present and one elects to be absent, he will learn to deal with that loss either in the family or in therapy, but it is not your place to anticipate the outcome by manipulating and alienating.

Some of you, and you know who you are, might believe that if you make your spouse appear disinterested or uninvolved with the children, you will seem more of an exemplary parent. This is faulty and dangerous thinking. Why not just be an exemplary parent and hope that your spouse does the same? How wonderful for your children to have two parents who are involved and interested in their lives rather than just one parent who is pulling along a wagon filled with boastful whining about how you have to do everything because the person you married is so lame. That works for a while, but soon all you are is a predictably alienating whiner.

If you want to punish your spouse and are thinking about poisoning the well with nasty comments about his laziness and irresponsibility, remember that words spoken resonate and eventually reach the wrong ears—the first being those of your children and the second those of the judge.

No matter how much you wish your spouse would vanish, it is likely you will be in his company in one way or another for quite a while. He will undoubtedly attend your children's graduations, toast their weddings, celebrate the birth of their babies, and hold their hands in times of tragedy. You are forever linked with this individual through your offspring, and if you can make that link pleasant, all of you will reap the benefits.

Few life experiences are more hurtful than finding out that your spouse has fallen out of love with you or fallen in love with someone else. It is devastating and unfair, but in our experience this news is usually the catalyst for alienation by the rejected parent. That your spouse has moved on has nothing to do with his attachment to his children, and you should not punish him for rejecting you by poisoning the children against him. Regardless of his moral character or his inability to follow through on his wedding vows, he does not have to be the enemy. In fact, he may be doing you a favor, because somewhere further on your life's journey you may find the love of your life as a result of his abandonment. But first things first. He is divorcing you, not the children. You are hurt, injured, traumatized, angry, enraged, betrayed, shattered, but you will regroup and recover. Your children may also feel emotions of hurt and betrayal, but mostly they just want everything to be okay. They will be far more forgiving in a far shorter time than you will because that is the miraculous nature of children, so let them grieve and let them recover without adding your own set of injuries to their confusion.

They want to be with the other parent just as much as they want to be with you. It is not a contest. They love you both, for different reasons and in different ways, but be assured that even a child who says he hates his parent does not. They need to talk, to express their feelings, to share their disappointment and their fears, but they do not need you to commiserate with them. That only causes them to stifle their words and feelings, because they know they still love the other parent regardless of the infraction. If you really want to help your children, encourage them to be with the estranged parent and remind them of how much they are loved by both of you. They will remember this gesture of kindness and wisdom for the rest of their lives.

CHAPTER FOURTEEN

So I Have to Be Nice?

No one expects children to be raised by morally unfit parents, and the courts are no exception. Unfortunately, in the mud-slinging that occurs in nasty divorces, this is usually one of the first accusations in custody battles. Making a spouse appear to be morally unfit due to substance abuse, including alcohol or drug usage or dependency, is a very serious matter, but also quite common. Think about it from the court's point of view. In marriages lasting years and years, neither party may have ever accused the other of moral unfitness; in fact, the accusing spouse may have allowed their children to be in the custody of the "unfit" parent on a daily basis: in the home, in the automobile, on vacation and the like. But suddenly "moral unfitness" surfaces and the accusations fly.

Are we really to believe that you spent the last five years of your life playing bridge across town while the children were in the custody of your spouse or that you encouraged him to transport the children to all the away baseball games but now you suddenly realize the danger they may be in because of that same spouse's moral unfitness? It just doesn't add up, but still it must be dealt with, and since it is your money, the attorneys will be happy to duke this one out in the courtroom if that's what you want.

Along with substance abuse, a favorite claim of moral unfitness is "sexual inappropriateness," meaning that a parent subjects his minor children to inappropriate material, philosophies, or people from whom they will learn immoral behaviors or ideas. This claim may hold more water because often during separation spouses may engage in activities that are questionable, such as the use of pornography, careless dating, immoral role modeling, and improper language. It's true that during a marriage some of these behaviors may have been hidden from the spouse but become overt with the freedom of separation and divorce. However, if you are making accusations about immorality or moral unfitness, be prepared to back up your statements with documented facts and evidence. Judges are not amused by theatrics of jealous and otherwise immature spouses who have decided to cast the other parent in a negative light without hard black and white facts. The burden of proof is on you.

While we're at it, might we remind you that you shouldn't throw stones if you live in a glass house. It's amazing how many parents point fingers while they themselves are indulging in the same nasty behaviors. Be fair in your concerns. If your spouse ties one on during a Tuesday night poker game and he doesn't have the children on that particular night, he is entitled to his private life, but if the children live with or visit your spouse and are exposed to alcohol, drugs, or hard-core pornography and gambling, you have a real issue.

On the flip side, if you consider your occupation as an escort or call girl to be professional and moral, you will be under scrutiny from the court, so be prepared. We're not making moral judgments about anyone's ability to make a living, but there are occupations upon which society frowns, especially where children are involved, and judges are members of society.

It's interesting to note that parents do less finger-pointing if the other spouse has not found a new love interest, so again, simplify your life by leaving out dating for now. However, for those of you who simply can't wait to get back into circulation, a word of wisdom. Your children do not want to know about your dating habits. They don't want to know that their other parent was so easily kicked to the curb. They don't want to see you and your new beau having any type of physical contact or engaging in eyeball gazing, because they think that it's embarrassing and gross. Your argument, no doubt—and we've heard it a thousand times—is that your children need to see affection between two people who are in love. Yes and no. It would have been great if that affection could have been demonstrated between you and your spouse, but it is not appropriate to be demonstrative with anyone else this early in the game.

Your children are going to feel a sense of loyalty to the other parent which precludes their aligning themselves with your new love interest. All you're doing is complicating the issue. They will want to spend time with you, but probably not with you and your friend. You won't want them to feel left out and therefore will try to include them in activities involving your date. Your date will feel like the children don't want to be there, and that's an accurate assessment. You will feel like you want to defend your date from the rudeness of your children, further escalating the situation. Take it from us. This is not going to work out the way you're hoping it will, so keep your love life and your parenting life separate for at least one year.

Before we put this topic to rest, we need to reiterate that your children are not dumb. They know what you're up to, especially in the bedroom. They hear through walls, they read sign language, they are more worldly than you know. Keep this relationship on the up and up. No child wants to imagine their parent involved in any sexual behavior and that feeling may last for years. If you can't control your impulses, at least take it away from the house and the children.

No one likes to be compared to someone else, but that is exactly what your spouse will do when he discovers he has been replaced by your new significant other, and he will not be pleased. Undoubtedly, this will fuel the fire of his concern about your judgment and the character of the person to whom you're subjecting your offspring. Try to be somewhat understanding. He has a right to be concerned, especially since your boyfriend may end up spending more time with his children than he does. There's enough room for everyone in this equation, but easing people in and out must be done delicately and tactfully.

Or maybe it's you who doesn't like the new girlfriend, especially if you believe the relationship began long before the marriage ended. No one could blame you for your disdain, but a word of caution: This woman may become the stepmother of your children. There is nothing you can do about that. For our money, you're better off having her as a friend than an enemy. While you're feeling all unhappy and off balance, it might be good to remember that no one will ever take your place. You are the biological parent and the person your children will love unconditionally and unequivocally. The "other woman" can never walk in your shoes; she knows it and you know it. Give her a break. She will have to try a lot harder with much less reward to gain the affection of your children. You have to do nothing except love them.

CHAPTER FIFTEEN

Enough, Already

The capacity and disposition of the parents to provide the children with food, clothing, shelter and medical care is essential to custody. For children to grow and develop in a healthy and safe manner they must be provided with, at the very least, a safe place to live, healthy nutrition, clothing that is appropriate, and healthcare, including medical, dental and eye. We tend to forget that our children are just babies, even those who may have passed puberty. They have little experience with which to steer their lives and they continue to count on you to help them learn.

Children need to be nurtured and pampered. If they're sick, they should be taken care of in a kind and compassionate manner. Working parents are under about as much pressure as most people can tolerate, but try not to view your sick children as more of an inconvenience than a concern. They are more important than losing a paycheck or avoiding the guilt your employer may try to place on your shoulders. When children are not feeling well they need a parent to watch over them if at all possible. They should not be left at home alone with a high fever or diarrhea. They should not be put to bed with abdominal pain or a severe headache because you have to get up for work in the morning. Their health is at issue, and their health comes first. Children can and do develop serious physical conditions. If you can't stay home with your sick child, ask your spouse if he can, or have a responsible neighbor or grandparent come over. Worst case scenario, call your local nursing/companion service and find a suitable "surrogate mother" or health provider until you get home.

Before you leave your child with an alternate caregiver, write down all medical information such as medicines, dosages, times and instructions; for example, "to be taken with food." Know your facts about healthcare and instruct your sitter accordingly. If your child must alternate Tylenol and Advil, be specific about the consequences of too much Tylenol on a small child's liver. If your child has chicken pox, know that you are never to administer aspirin either during, or for some time following, the disease in order to prevent the grave consequences of Reye's Syndrome. In the event that your caretaker makes an error with the medication or the dosage, instruct them to call the Poison Control Center, whose number you've provided, or take the child to the nearest emergency room. With some medications, even a single wrong dosage may be life-threatening. For obvious reasons, children should never be allowed to administer their own medications until they are of sound reason, which is probably as long as they are living under your roof.

Most of all, believe your children if they say they don't feel well. Take their temperature. Look at their eyes. Don't send them to school if they are genuinely too ill to be out of bed, and if you do send them, be available to pick them up at a moment's notice if they become worse. Children can get very sick at an amazingly rapid rate, but they can also bounce back quickly. Still, not every illness is "just a cold," and each one should be treated with respect.

Children should not have to fear the house or the neighborhood in which they live. Not only should they have heat in winter, windows that latch, a roof that doesn't leak and indoor plumbing, but they should feel the sense of "home" after a long day at school. The house should be clean. Notice we did not say sanitized, but clean. A messy house when there are children living in it is to be expected, but an overly messy house not only breeds dust and dirt but can also be a fire hazard in the middle of the night. Accidents occur when things are left lying about: a dropped shoe here, a roller skate there. Help your children learn to manage their things by observing you managing yours.

If you believe as most parents do that children should have chores, make sure that the chores you dole out are appropriate and that you aren't pushing your housework onto them. It is not their job to clean your house. The argument, "They live here, too," falls short. We've already made the point that, until they pay the rent or mortgage, children do not have a final say in making decisions. You can't have it both ways. It's your house. You make the final decisions, which are hopefully in the best interest of the family. Those decisions should not include making the children do the laundry, housework and cooking. We know you're tired and you could use some help, but not at their expense.

Well then, what are appropriate chores? Assuming that we're talking about children who have reached adolescence or young adulthood, it is perfectly acceptable for them to help set and clear the table, load the dishwasher, take out the garbage, and clean their room. Perhaps you could use a team effort regarding housework. While you vacuum the living room, your child could dust the furniture, but it is not acceptable for them to have the responsibility of cleaning whole rooms. Should they clean the bathroom after themselves? That would be nice. It probably won't happen, but it would be nice. Should they feed the dog? Sure, why not? But don't count on it getting done in a timely manner, and you'd better check to see if it has been done at all. We're pretty much in agreement that chores are better left to taking care of things that don't need to eat and breathe while your children are still in the process of learning responsibility.

As long as we're talking about chores, we might as well talk about allowances, although no one will ever agree on what is an acceptable amount, whether children should be paid to do chores, and the like. On the plus side, receiving an allowance is certainly a good way to learn the concept of money and how to budget. On the negative side, children should not have to forego activities with their friends because they could not properly manage their money. Neither can you, and you still manage to go out with your friends.

Children should not have the financial burden of purchasing their own clothing, hygiene products, school supplies or lunch. They should be given a certain amount of money to participate in activities but not so much that you feel you are employed by and working for them. Money can be stretched only so far, and children have to learn the concept of a dollar. On the other hand, we have seen plenty of families where the money flows pretty freely for parental purchases without allotting anything for the offspring. While we have already stated our feeling that children and parents are never placed on equal levels, fair is fair, and your children should have a place in the shopping mix. We can hear your shouts of protest over your children's sheer laziness when it comes to taking care of their clothing. We know that. Children trade clothes, leave their winter coats in the bushes at the curb before they get on the bus, cut off pants legs and sleeves, and commit lots of other clothing infractions, but that's the nature of the beast. You were young once. How much of your parents' hard-earned money did you waste by losing or loaning your clothing?

You and your children will never come to a meeting of the minds on what clothing is appropriate and how much that clothing should cost, but be as generous as you can. Remember, it wasn't so long ago that you were using the same arguments with your parents. Clothing, or the lack of the "right" clothing, does put your child in a certain category of popularity with his peers, and although unfair, in the subculture of teenage school yard society, the person with shabby clothing will be singled out for humiliation. Some parents believe that it's perfectly all right to send their children off to the mall with a credit card in their pocket. We don't know how responsible your children are, but most kids won't necessarily stay on task or budget. If you've ever observed the clothing of adolescents walking the corridors of malls and wondered what their parents were thinking when they took their kids shopping, consider the possibility that they may not have been present when the purchases were made.

Activities are another huge money pit, but if your children want to go bowling or to the local movie theater, they will need money in their pocket. In addition to the cost of the activity, they will need at a minimum a snack and a drink. Until they're sixteen they should not work and generally aren't legally able to collect a paycheck, so they're pretty much dependent on you for their entertainment, clothing and the like. This is not to say that they should get the latest model two-hundred-dollar sneakers, but neither should they be embarrassed about their footwear.

If you are receiving child support, don't count on that being enough to provide for your child. It will not be enough. You will have to put some money in the kitty as well. It is difficult to determine just how many salaries it takes to support even one child, but the numbers are astounding. It is not their fault. There are school functions, after-school activities, braces, cars, band, ski club, senior trips, school pictures, science projects, haircuts, doctor visits, lost library books, traffic tickets, college applications. The list is endless. Children are expensive, with no end in sight. That's the reason most parents do not even dream the words "early retirement."

Just a short note on food. It's great that Junior is happy to eat fast food every day, but that option is neither nutritious nor feasible if having healthy children is one of your goals. On the other hand, most children are not up to eating three-course meals every day and do not appreciate the amount of time you slaved over a standing rib roast. They simply want to eat what is fast and available and tastes good. Compliments to the chef will come about ten or fifteen years from now, when they miss your cooking. Don't grow old waiting.

We're really trying to get back on track with all the divorce issues, but we can hear concerns about what you might consider your children's rudeness and lack of appreciation for all you do, so once again we will digress for a moment. Children are appreciative in their own way. Contrary to what you hear from their own little mouths, your children know they have it pretty good, and in another decade they'll be submitting your name for sainthood. But they have to pass the normal childhood milestones just as you once did, and part of that process is feeling like they're being treated unfairly, their life sucks, they got stuck with the worst parents and no one understands them. Such is life.

CHAPTER SIXTEEN

There is Nothing Funny about This

Domestic violence is an immature, cowardly, angry act of aggression which should never occur at all but certainly should not occur more than once without immediate resolution of the problem. We are supposed to learn as children that there are better outlets for frustration than inflicting physical harm on another human being, and if we haven't learned that lesson at home by the time we reach school-age, it will be a much harder lesson to learn later. There is no amount of annoyance, nagging, ignorance or betrayal that excuses this type of physical altercation, and certainly it should never occur in the presence of minor children.

We continue to try to teach lessons to our kids without giving them proper role modeling and imprinting. If your children have ever witnessed domestic violence between you and your spouse and you have not taken immediate action such as reporting the abuse to the authorities, they have already learned a powerful negative message: that it is all right to strike out physically in anger. Children are naturally fearful young people who look toward their parents for safety and security. Just as we don't promote other crimes, we cannot be lackadaisical about domestic abuse. It is not all right to hit, punch, strike, push, pinch or shove another human being—ever.

If you are confused about this, if you have reservations about what to do in a situation involving domestic battery, if you believe for one moment that it won't happen again, you are dead wrong. The number of domestic violence incidents is on the rise, either because it is now being recognized and treated as the crime it is, or because societal stressors have increased anger and decreased frustration tolerance. Either way, there is no excuse for this mismanagement of anger, and no reason to believe that battery will end after one incident.

Domestic violence occurs not only between husband and wife but can also involve other family members. When it involves a parent and child it is usually termed child abuse. When we strike out at our children, we are role modeling the inability to deal with problems from a calm and unemotional stance. Let's face it, parents do hit their children; quite frankly, for decades it was more the rule than the exception. However, regardless of your personal beliefs pro or con spanking, there are laws that protect children from this type of behavior, and if you should be turned into the authorities you might be surprised to find that the offense is taken quite seriously.

There are certainly plenty of parents trained in old-school thinking who blame sparing the rod with spoiling the child, and we have only to look at the changing societal mores regarding children and the lack of discipline to agree that something must be done, but "striking sense" into a child is not the answer. If your spouse has been hitting or otherwise abusing your child and you have not interceded, you are also guilty of child endangerment, so we really should get this straight. No one should hit a child. Children misbehave, they are rude and disrespectful, they are willful and annoying when they want to be, and usually that is during times when you have enough on your plate already. But children are supposed to be all of the above when they don't get their way or they're tired or hungry or just feeling miserable. That's why they're called children.

Adults, on the other hand, are not children, and the same set of rules does not apply to both. When you are feeling tired, hungry or miserable, you're going to have to find some way of dealing with your stress without taking it out on the children. If your spouse cannot control his impulses because he's had a bad day or a bad year, you must ensure their safety by clueing him in about the emotional and legal facts of child abuse and if that doesn't work removing either him or you and the children from the home. Under no circumstances can you turn your back on what is going on right in front of you. We have treated parents who feigned ignorance or stated that they "weren't at home" or "don't know anything about that" when faced with their children finally getting the attention of an adult who called a child protection agency.

Being unaware of what's happening in your children's lives and being unavailable to them is not being a good parent. It's just that simple. If you continue to pretend not to know what you do know, you will begin to see your children acting out in aggressive, hostile ways that will be difficult to disarm. Step in and do the right thing, even if it means the end of your marriage. Your children cannot protect themselves without your assistance. Don't lie for your partner under any circumstances. If he's a "great guy" except for the anger, then guess what? He's not a great guy!

If you are the person being battered, you must notify the authorities and allow them to take the offender away. We know that he may be the primary breadwinner in the household, but that doesn't give him a free pass. If you have to move in with your family, take in a roommate, work two jobs and downsize, it is all worth it for your safety and that of your children.

This seems pretty easy on paper, but it's much more difficult in real life. For one thing, you are feeling off balance as a result of your spouse's attack, but for a moment let's retrace some steps and find out just how we've come to this point. Husbands or wives do not just arrive overnight at a place in their relationship where physical battery occurs. It happens as a result of a deep-seated rage which begins to show itself early in the relationship. This rage is not always directed at you, but it is present just the same. It's not uncommon for women to say their husbands seem to be "on a short fuse," especially when alcohol or drugs are involved. They may also indicate that there were precipitating factors, such as a colicky baby or loss of a job. Perhaps there are teenagers in the household exerting their own belligerent independence that has caused a loss of control. But these are all excuses.

Even when things were going well, try to recall incidents when out of nowhere your spouse began a verbal rampage of put-downs to purposefully demean you or expose your weaknesses. The first verbal abusive experience is almost always the worst, leaving the targeted spouse feeling emotionally betrayed and distraught. After a while, you come to anticipate verbal abuse and expect insinuations and sarcasm to be hurled your way, but you've learned to protect yourself as best you can by building an invisible wall of armor to surround you so that you are immune to the insults, or think you are. But you are not deaf, and words spoken are words forever. They hurt. They cause you to second-guess yourself and have misgivings about what part you might be playing in your spouse's frustration, until finally you begin to feel quite badly about yourself. You are not happy, but you have been isolated and drained of your resources, and without supportive family and friends, you begin to spiral into helplessness. You try harder. You apologize. You make promises to do better, all the while knowing that the offenses for which you are now taking responsibility are not yours.

Once you have shouldered some of the responsibility for your spouse's bad behavior, the door opens for escalation of his anger and rage. He can't respect you because of your lack of backbone and weakness, even though your previous strength angered him as well. There is no winning here. You have now entered the world of abuse.

From the outside looking in, it's very easy for people to make simplistic suggestions, such as "Just leave" or "Why don't you just stand up to it?" But to the victim of abuse the situation looks so overwhelmingly hopeless there seems nowhere to turn. An adept abuser has already isolated his victim from friends and family, and she doesn't want to expose her failed relationship or her weakness to estranged friends. A further complication is that many victims have a need to protect the abusive spouse from the outside world because if she doesn't leave him she doesn't want anyone to think badly of either of them. How the family unit is perceived by the outside world weighs heavily in the mind of the victim, and she will pay whatever it costs to protect the image of a happy family.

Like children, adult victims also worry that no one will believe them or that they will be accused of overreacting. Usually, the abusive spouse is able to control his angry outbursts and cynical remarks in public and is, in fact, often well-liked and considered "the life of the party." He portrays himself as a martyr who is saddled with a depressed and miserable spouse and is often spoken about in heroic whispers by neighbors and friends.

That said, if you are battered verbally, emotionally, physically or sexually, you must get out immediately for the safety and well-being of yourself and your children, because abusive behavior will intensify until the slap becomes a punch and the beating becomes death.

It would be easy to leave an abusive spouse if only they were consistently abusive, but they're too clever for that, intermittently being warm and tender, offering loving promises and gifts. The apologies and tears appear to be heartfelt, and the begging for another chance could melt a heart of stone. But these are the facts. Without psychological therapy and anger management treatment, and often despite therapy and treatment, these abusers will continue their pattern of abuse fueled by deep-seated hostility and the rage of unresolved childhood, interpersonal, or family conflicts. Most of the rage is not about you but is misdirected at you. Since you are not the underlying source of the rage, nothing you can do will resolve the problem.

Once you take a stand and call the authorities, do not back down. Take pictures of your bruises, solicit neighbors and friends to witness your injuries, document the details of the incident not only in police reports but also in detailed logs to be brought to the judge. Get a restraining order. Do not bail him out of jail. Do not feel sorry for him because he has to be at work, because his parents will be upset, because the children don't want their daddy in jail. You didn't start this, but you have the ability to end it once and for all. He doesn't believe you will follow through, especially when he begs and pleads for one more chance. He will twist and manipulate the facts and ask how you could do this to him, how you could take him from his children. He will tell you that without you and the kids he has nothing. He will threaten suicide. Do not back down.

Domestic violence has come into its own in the past decade with televised celebrity exposure and stiffer laws protecting victims of crime. In many states a call to the authorities involving domestic violence will culminate in the abuser being handcuffed and taken to jail. He will usually be able to bond out the next day, with a scheduled court appearance in the future. He will undoubtedly get legal assistance. He will hope you drop the charges. Most states now release the victim from the responsibility of having to prosecute by making domestic violence a crime against the state. Even if the victim withdraws the complaint, the abuser may be tried and sentenced by the state.

No one should be alone with an abuser—not you and not your children. If you don't have a place to go, your community has facilities to put you and the children in a temporary safe environment. The location of these facilities is not publicized for reasons of safety, but the police will escort you there if needed. If you have time to pack, bring personal hygiene products, changes of clothing, medications, important papers, bottles and diapers, schoolbooks, and any other essentials you need to get you through the next few days, weeks or months. If you don't have time to pack or don't want to call attention to your leaving, you will be given essentials at the facility that your community has deemed "safe" and protected by both location and confidentiality, and escorted home at a later time by police to gather your personal belongings or to move back into the marital home if your spouse has been ordered to leave.

Verbal and physical abusers are used to controlling other people. Their manipulations and other tactics have worked quite well for them in the past, and they don't expect this dysfunctional lifestyle to be interrupted or terminated. Don't underestimate yourself. You must help the police and court system to help you in stopping this cycle of abuse. We're aware that there are some abusers who will not go away whatever the cost, who will retaliate regardless of a restraining order, and whom you should fear. However, the abusive behavior would have escalated regardless of anything you did or did not do, and for the most part these emotionally immature and disturbed people will set their sights on another victim who is not as strong as you have become.

On the flip side of actual domestic violence are fabricated accusations of domestic violence for the purposes of discrediting a spouse and ensuring that the children will be awarded to the nonviolent parent. Unfortunately, there are far too many of these false accusations clogging up the courtrooms. It takes a pretty desperate person to use these kinds of manipulative, twisted, unfair and deceptive tactics. If you are alleging prior abuse and there are no pictures, police records, witnesses and the like, you will have to stretch pretty far to find an interested party in the judicial system, but if the allegations are recent and the wounds self-inflicted or the events staged, you will be up against quite a battle. No self-respecting spouse is going to sit back while you make spousal abuse accusations. He will have to retain a criminal attorney, and that attorney is going to punch all kinds of holes in your story, but only after thousands of family dollars have been spent trying to prove and disprove these claims.

If you are found to have filed false statements to the court, you will be guilty of perjury, which is a crime that will earn you jail time. You will also be disqualified from consideration as residential custodial parent, as well you should be.

CHAPTER SEVENTEEN

Or This

There is almost nothing more heinous than the crime of sexual abuse of a child. It rattles the very core of decency and shakes the foundation of security. Sexual abuse of a child by his own parent or stepparent is a despicable act committed by a very sick individual. It is incest and it is wrong. The horror of suspecting that your child has been abused sexually by your spouse is horrific and surreal, and many parents blame themselves for not being more aware or more protective. Discovery of such an act will change the thinking of any parent forever.

Now imagine how it must feel to be the recipient of that sexual abuse—what it must be like for a child who has been cruelly plucked out of childhood and exposed to humiliation, pain, fear and injury. If there is any question about the magnitude of the damage done to the victims subjected to such horrendous trauma, let us assure you that the very fiber of a child's being has been permanently altered, with behavioral and emotional consequences that almost certainly will manifest later in life as dysfunction in interpersonal intimacy and relationships.

A sexual abuser is a coward. He is no higher than an animal and has no more integrity than a psychopath. There will be no remorse to protect the next victim. Even hardened criminals have no use for pedophiles, no use for someone who preys on the helplessness of children. Sexual abuse may run the gamut from "wrestling" games to outright fondling, from bathroom voyeurism to oral sex or intercourse. It may be argued that these abusers are sick, and we will argue that is not a good enough excuse, not when children are damaged, not when families are torn apart, not when lives are ruined.

Worse than finding out that your child has been victimized by your spouse is having suspected it and done nothing. You are your child's link to the outside world, you are the person who has the intellect and resources to summon assistance, you are the person who has chosen to put your child in danger if you suspected abuse and chose to do nothing about it.

When children of abuse become adults, their memories may be blurred, their senses dulled by a brain smart enough to shield them from the vivid recollection of the trauma, but there will be pieces, fragments, comet tails of memories that prevent the past from ever being put to rest. These vaguely recalled scenarios of abuse will include anger at the perpetrator or, unbelievably, forgiveness. They will also include some measure of self-blame as the child tries to rearrange remembered incidents so he can view himself as fighting back, or at least making the effort to fight back. Some of the scenarios the child's mind produces will involve you, the parent who knew and did nothing, or who didn't know but should have known. There will be a sense of loss and grief for their shattered innocence and for the loss of trust of the very parent who professes to love them.

If you suspect anything at all that seems out of the ordinary, do not discount your intuition. You must err on the side of caution and sharpen your focus on everything from body language to overt sexual comments made by your spouse. If your spouse has obsessions with unorthodox sexual stimulation, especially if that stimulation comes from the Internet, where "kiddy porn" can be downloaded, you must take immediate steps to remove yourself and your children from his presence. In this case, act first and gather evidence later, because waiting too long is often just that . . . waiting too long!

If your children or stepchildren exhibit behavioral signs that arouse suspicion of sexual abuse, deal with them immediately. If your usually happy child becomes withdrawn or depressed, shows signs of agitation or fear, or becomes clingy or angry, take notice. In younger children, especially those who cannot adequately express themselves, there may be crying in response to irritation around the anal or vaginal areas, there may be excessive masturbation or a need to fondle their genitals. They may have changes in their appetite or sleep patterns and frequent waking with nightmares. In older children there may be promiscuity and self-destructive behaviors such as cutting, substance abuse, and involvement in destructive relationships. In children of all ages there may be somatic complaints such as headaches and stomachaches of unknown cause.

These behaviors do not have a short shelf life. They follow the victims into their relationships, into their marriages, and into their private and intimate moments, causing marital dysfunction, orgasmic disorders, gender confusion, lack of trust, feelings of helplessness, difficulty with authority figures, dysfunctional parenting, and choice of partners who need to be "saved" or "rescued."

You have responsibilities to educate your children about what is proper and what is not, beginning with youngsters and their introduction to "good touching" and "bad touching." You should assure them that nothing they ever tell you will make you angry at them or make you stop loving them so that the doors of communication stay open. That said, if your child suggests or directly tells you that their other parent or anyone else has made them feel "uncomfortable," even if nothing happened, you must act like a jailhouse warden, putting everyone in lockdown until each and every person and action involved is accounted for to your satisfaction. Your child needs to know that behind your words are serious, aggressive actions that will assure them of protection.

If your child is pubescent or adolescent or, for that matter, even a young adult, know that sex with a parent or stepparent is incest. Even if your spouse tells you that the child consented to sexual activity, we are here to tell you unequivocally that there is no such thing as sexual consent between a minor child and an adult. End of story. That parent must be prosecuted the same as if your child was six instead of sixteen. The marriage is over, the spouse has no further contact with the children unless supervised, and the courts will determine when and if that will occur.

Some of you, thankfully the minority, will actually consider dating a sexual offender even though you have minor children living in your household. Do not do that! We don't care how much you love each other or how sorry you feel for him because he got a "bum rap," you cannot take a chance that his "rehabilitation" is worth the amount of copper in a penny. Most states do not allow sexual offenders to be within a specified number of feet of minor children, schools or playgrounds, and they do that for good reason. Do not bring such people into your family's life.

As with domestic violence, suspected sexual abuse calls for immediate action. If you don't notify the authorities, someone else who has contact with your child and knowledge of the abuse—school personnel, your doctor, a therapist—will turn that information over to your state's Department of Children and Families or other appropriate agency. If you have glossed over the urgency of calling the authorities, your behavior will be scrutinized as well. Just because you aren't the abuser doesn't mean you won't be charged with neglect if you withhold information.

If your child has been molested in any way, he or she will have to speak with detectives to document the events as the child remembers them. They will also be examined by a medical doctor for emotional and physical evidence of molestation. Often there are no overt physical signs of abuse, but that does not discount its occurrence. There are also times when the child solicits the abuser to perform the sexual acts rather than vice versa. This is still incest.

Once documented, your divorce attorney, and we hope you, will run, not walk, to your spouse's divorce attorney and make the judge aware of the allegations and eventual findings. Suffice it to say, this child will never reside with the abusive parent.

Following this type of emotional and/or physical trauma, your child will be in absolute need of professional help by a seasoned therapist who can help them rebuild their life without guilt. Even if your child seems fine, or they are adamant about not wanting to relive the experiences through therapy, they cannot be allowed to make that decision for themselves. It is rare, if ever, that someone will be able to resolve an incestuous violation without professional assistance. We must state that you as a parent should not hold your child responsible in any way for the sexual involvement. There are some individuals who cannot believe their spouse would be involved in such sordid activity without being "lured" into sex by the provocativeness of the child. No child, even a scantily dressed, suggestively talking adolescent, can lure a mature healthy adult into anything that remotely resembles incest.

CHAPTER EIGHTEEN

🦋 *Kid Wisdom*

Unless a court-ordered evaluation is requested, it is best to try to keep children uninvolved in the actual divorce process. They do not need to be made aware of the details of allegations, nor of the cost of attorney fees and the like. However, if a court does order an evaluation by a forensic psychologist or a psychologist specially trained in the field of divorce and legal matters, the costs may become quite steep. Usually these psychologists are paid at an hourly rate ranging from two- to three-hundred dollars per hour, and most will expect a retainer of several thousand dollars before they begin their investigation and evaluation.

Depending on how complex a case is—how much paperwork and documentation must be read and digested, how much time it takes to visit with each parent individually and with their children and then with the children individually—there may be many hours involved, as there should be for rendering such a life-changing decision as which parent will make the better residential custodial parent. This decision is not made lightly, nor is it made quickly. Often, members of the family are called back again and again to see how things fit together or fall apart. Initially, most adults have excellent presentation, but eventually normal personalities and interactions manifest, allowing the forensic psychologist to view the family as it normally functions.

Children present the most genuinely of all the members of the family; their agenda is simply "to get this over with" so they can get back home to play or watch television. Many children will share their views of what has gone wrong between their parents, and it's amazing how much information they've been fed by the very adults that should be shielding them. Children barely able to read will recite chapter and verse of how one parent "cheated" on the other, using words like "affair" and "sex" with age inappropriateness.

The history of the parents' involvement with their children, the manner in which the parents and children bond with each other, information identifying the parent who has been the most nurturing and most hands-on with regard to taking the children to the doctor and dentist, attending school conferences, and helping with homework are all taken into consideration. The parent deemed to have the ability to maintain the most stable home environment—financially, physically, and emotionally—will generally be awarded residential custody.

There are creative ways of deciding residential custody when there are two equally acceptable parents. The children can remain in the marital home while the parents move in and out weekly. If Mom and Dad live in the same neighborhood and school district, the children can alternate houses, living at Mom's house one week and Dad's the next. Better still, there can be an open-door policy, with parents living next door or in close proximity to each other while the children have the benefit of both households and both parents. Any and all of these possibilities exist provided the parents are willing to work together to put the interests of the children first and foremost.

CHAPTER NINETEEN

Light Reading

We have addressed most of what the court system will be concerned with if and when you come before a judge in child custody battles. Depending on the state in which you reside, you are likely to encounter some or most of the following and may want to use this checklist as a guide.

1) Which parent shows the most willingness to keep the lines of communication open and encourage contact with the nonresidential parent?

2) Which parent seems to be the most emotionally stable?

3) Which parent evidences the most moral fitness?

4) Which parent possesses the better mental and physical health?

5) Which parent can offer more permanence with regard to preserving the family as a unit?

6) Whom do the children seem to bond with by way of nurturing and preference?

7) Which parent is most likely to be able to provide food, clothing, shelter, medical care and other necessities?

8) Which parent has the more involvement with and interest in school, community, and home activities?

9) Which parent most encourages a close parent-child relationship with the other parent?

10) Is there evidence of domestic violence, and if so, by whom?

11) Is there evidence of sexual abuse, and if so, by whom?

12) Any other relevant facts which should be made known to the court.

CHAPTER TWENTY

Acceptance and Other Sorrows

We remind you that loving your children is only half the battle. The other half involves educating yourself in parenting skills, being present and available to meet your children's needs, and admitting error. We understand that you have made mistakes along the way. All of us have. No one is going to demote you if you admit your mistakes and ask for assistance, but if your parenting skills are less than they should be and you continue making the same mistakes expecting different results, that's a different story. Why not begin right now, today, to give your children the best possible start in life by creating a loving, consistent household which includes both parents? Divorce does not mean an end to your parental relationship, nor will it benefit you or your children to alienate them from either parent. Maturity must be demonstrated before it can be achieved. You are the example of what you hope to instill in your children. We say that if you want a predictor of future behavior, look to the parents before you look to the children.

Let's step into the lives of a family that might seem familiar, perhaps even reminding you of your own, and examine some of the personality factors and family dynamics that culminate in divorce and see how one family learned to solve their interpersonal relationship for the sake of the children. The dialogue chronicling the experience of Carl, the husband, denoted by regular print, and Emily, the wife, denoted by italicized print, is fictionalized and does not represent real individuals.

I think I dreamed about being someone's wife for most of my childhood. I loved the idea of belonging to a man who would adore and cherish me, the way my father adored and cherished my mother. I used to spend much of my classroom time scribbling my name on my book covers and matching up the last names of potential suitors, which at that time would be almost any boy in my class, just to see how our names fit together. Like a painter with a clean canvas, I began mentally sketching our lives together. He would be tall and very handsome, with a deep voice that was both soothing and protective. He would find me beautiful and talented and would be unable to contain his love for and devotion to me. We would have two children, a boy and a girl, who would be the spitting image of each of us, possessing all of our strengths and none of our weaknesses. Friends and family would marvel at how our love was written in the stars, validating its eternal nature to everyone who knew us.

I never understood women, never could trust them. My mother was the type of woman who made a lot of promises but didn't keep most of them. She was a good woman, but just totally disorganized; she lost things, things that embarrassed me in front of my teachers, like my permission slips for field trips or my lunch money. She had to be reminded over and over about the dates of my baseball practices or my school activities. Once she even forgot to pick me up after a five-day ski trip with my junior high school ski club. I mean, there I was, the last kid in the parking lot, waiting with a teacher for his mom. I vowed right then and there that I wasn't going to count on her anymore, and once I got my driver's license I pretty much didn't have to, but still, I missed some of the special moments that other kids had and I didn't. One thing in particular stands out in my mind, even though it's been more than twenty years. I got lucky enough to get a prom date with the most popular girl in the class. I couldn't believe it! My sister helped me order the wrist corsage and my tuxedo. I paid for it with the money I made waiting tables, and I was happy to do it. I would have spent every last dime just to go on that date. When the night of the dance came, I walked down the stairs in my tux and waited for my mom to straighten my tie. She told me to come back with my date and she would take special pictures of us, and she did, my arm around the most beautiful girl in the whole school, her head leaning on my shoulder, my arms around her waist, her gazing into my eyes. She took twenty-four pictures in all, and to tell you the truth, I don't know if I was more excited to be seen with this girl at the prom or to have the pictures developed. The next day, when I went to take the film to the drugstore, the camera was empty, like some cruel joke. My mother had some lame excuse about thinking she loaded the camera when she hadn't, and tried to make light of it. My friends thought the story was hilarious, but that night I cried like I was a little baby. I cried not because it was my only date with that girl, but because I knew my mom would never understand how many times she had minimized my feelings and let me down.

When I first laid eyes on Carl, it was love at first sight. I was registering for classes my freshman year in college; he was playing a game of touch football on the campus with a bunch of his rowdy friends. He almost fell right into me, and I knew right then and there it was fate, that we were meant to be together. Looking back, it was probably me that ran after him, although I have never admitted that to anyone. He once said something about how I chased him and how he credits his running away from me to his first-place trophy in cross-country. It was a night that we had a few couples over for dinner, maybe after we had been married for a year or so, and it was the first major argument we ever had. I was just devastated, so humiliated to have everyone laugh at my expense. I tried to laugh it off too, and act like I was enjoying the joke, but when they left I really laid into him. I don't think I've ever forgiven him for saying those things in public, not because they were false, but because they were true.

Emily has always been really touchy and sensitive. She expects me to sit around and talk about feelings day in and day out. She loves to analyze every move we make, together and apart, but she talks about the same things over and over, like I'm some kind of moron who can't understand the English language. I get what she's saying, but I don't agree with it. She has some romanticized version of what she thinks our marriage should be, and quite frankly I can't live in her dreamworld anymore. She doesn't have any understanding of my job and doesn't seem to realize that because I own my own business, if I don't work there is no money. Somehow she thinks I can take her on all the vacations she wants and still have enough money left to pay the bills. It just doesn't work that way. I'm tired of her complaining about how oppressed she feels and how much she needs to get away. Maybe she should try working outside in the hot sun ten hours a day and then she might have reason to complain. She's had a cushy life, and one she doesn't appreciate. She wanted to have two kids; we had two kids. She wanted to live out in the country; we live out in the country. She wanted to be a stay-at-home mother; she quit her job and stayed home for the past ten years. Don't get me wrong, I don't begrudge those decisions. I'm just saying she's had a good life, but for her there is never an end to her misery.

My father offered Carl a job with his firm, promising him a job as vice-president. It was an unbelievable opportunity for us to get ahead, for us to make lots of money and have things that we always wanted, but Carl turned the job down. He said it was because he's not cut out for a nine-to-five job where he has to punch a time clock, but I think he just didn't want to work for my father. I mean, what kind of idiot turns down a spot in the family business? Well, that didn't win him any points with my parents, and I still can't believe all the things we can't do because of his limited salary. He just won't comply with anyone else's wishes. He's selfish and does whatever he wants without compromising. He says I can't let that go, that I constantly bring up our lack of money to punish him. Maybe I do punish him, but he deserves it. All he had to do was take the damn job and that would have been that.

Emily has never forgiven me for not allowing her father to control me. That's how I see it, anyway. He's used to making people tow the line at work because his wife nags him to death at home, so he pays it forward. I guess everyone has to control some aspect of his life, and more power to him if he gets off bossing people around at work, but he's not going to control me. I learned a long time ago to count on myself if I want to be in charge of me. Emily acts like we're heading for skid row. We have a beautiful house in a great neighborhood, the kids have never had to miss out on any activities because of a lack of money, and I've worked hard to put away money for their college education. Of course, because they're only twelve and eight, Emily doesn't give that college fund much credit. To her, the kids are going to be little forever, and college seems a million years away. She wants everything yesterday without the first clue as to how much it actually takes to run the household and save for our future. As far as she's concerned, I had the chance to make money, even though I would have been miserable, and she will never give that a rest.

Even though I love the girls, I probably wasn't ready to be a mother. My own mother had so much patience, it just seemed so easy for her. The way she seemed to have endless energy for us kids, the way she cleaned the house and put the meals on the table with such cheerfulness. I never once heard her complain about being trapped in the house or being tired of her life. She was just a born mother. Maybe because it seemed like such little effort, motherhood hit me pretty hard. I mean, I knew babies cried, but no matter what I did, they just never stopped. Being a mother has just drained me. Then I look at Carl and he seems to have a great life. He doesn't have to deal day in and day out with temper tantrums and stomach viruses, all he has to do is get up, go to work, come home, play with the girls a little and go to bed. I guess there is a part of me that resents his freedom, and I guess there is a part of me that wants the reward for all the work I do. I feel like I deserve to go on shopping sprees or vacations. By the time the girls are grown and out of the house I'll be too old to enjoy it.

For the past two years nothing I ever do is right, according to Emily. I don't spend enough time with her. I don't spend enough time with the girls. I come home too late at night, or I expect the house to be clean. Emily thinks my expectations of her are unreasonable, but the fact is, she's the one who's being unreasonable. What man comes home to find his house filthy dirty every day of the week, no hot dinner on the table, and his wife moaning about how difficult her day has been? She thinks I should come home and pick up the pieces the minute I walk in the door. She doesn't care about how my day went or whether I'm hungry or thirsty or sick. It's all about her, all the time. We argue and I try to show her how unfair she's being. Then she makes an attempt to clean the house or cook dinner for a few days before it all goes to hell. I look back now and see my mother all over again. Lots of promises with nothing to show for it. Nothing but a bunch of empty words that are worth a whole lot of nothing.

I admit to being a nag, but to me that's no reason for him to do what he did. When he said those wedding vows he promised that he would be faithful, but here we are eleven years married and what does he do? He cheats on me, that's what. He'll lie and say she's only a friend, but I wasn't born yesterday. It hurts me so bad that he could just replace me like that. I mean, here I've been picking up his dirty socks and underwear while somebody else got the fringe benefits. No wonder he hasn't touched me in six months; if he's getting it somewhere else, what does he need me for? My father wasn't surprised. He said, "If you sleep with dogs, expect to get fleas," and that's what I did. He said he knew from the beginning that Carl was no damn good, knew it as soon as he thought he was too good to take that job offer. He said if he has anything to say about it, he'll get me the best lawyer in the state to take him for everything.

I just can't believe this is happening. I mean, I know that makes no sense, considering what I've done, but I do love my wife. I just couldn't take it anymore, the feeling of not being appreciated and not being loved. She turned me down sexually almost every time I asked until I finally quit asking. There's only so much a man can take before other women start looking good. She was someone I knew from town. Just a friend, at least that's what I thought. It was nice to have someone to talk to who didn't analyze me, didn't criticize me, who laughed at my jokes and thought I was fun to be with. Let's face it, me and Emily haven't had fun in years. I'm not blaming her, I guess we just got ourselves in a rut, but this other woman was the exit on the highway to nowhere, the neon light on the rest stop to take you out of the rain. I never thought it would get to sex. I thought about it, I won't lie to you, but I'd have never done it if she hadn't come put it in my face. I mean, I'm a strong man, but I couldn't take it anymore.

I think about him with her all the time. I'm obsessed with the thought of them together, and I hate him for it. I imagine him buying her flowers, or staring into her eyes and listening to her all night long. When I think of him with her it makes me crazy. I want to hurt him, not physically but in some way like he's hurt me. Well, if you really want the truth, sometimes I wish I could hurt him physically, even though I would never do it, and this is coming from someone who can't even kill a fly. That's how angry and hurt I am. The worst is when I start to think of them in the bedroom. I try to push those thoughts away, but I can't. It's like I'm comparing her to me. Is her stomach flatter, are her breasts bigger, is she more aggressive in bed? The worst part about being cheated on is how it makes me feel about myself. I feel ugly and old and used up. I feel like no one else will ever want me because I had a husband who promised to love me and he couldn't, even though he had me at my best, my skinniest, and now I'm on a downhill spiral toward old age.

We tried to work it out with marriage counseling but she had me jumping through hoops. There was no pleasing her in therapy, just like there was no pleasing her at home. All she wanted to do was degrade me and attack me for being unfaithful. I admitted it was a lousy, hurtful thing to do, but it's time to get past the affair and try to work things out. When it was my turn and the therapist asked me what factors precipitated me straying from the marriage, she blew a gasket. She was in my face and then in his face and then accused both of us of having some kind of male conspiracy thing going. She finally walked out and hasn't been back since.

My friends told me that marriage counseling was going to be a waste of time if he didn't accept all the blame for the mess the marriage is in. They really got me riled up before I went into therapy, telling me not to accept any blame, not to seem too eager to put the marriage back together. They said after what he did to me and the kids he should crawl back to me, and even then not to give him much hope. I did what they said, and at the time it felt good, but now I wish I hadn't listened. What did I gain from all that power and control? No husband, that's what. No husband and no marriage. But at least I still have my friends, and they tell me they'll help me get through this divorce. They've already given me names of real "shark" attorneys who will go for the jugular. I can't believe things have gone this far, but I don't think I can turn back now. I want to, I really do. Sometimes I just want him to hold me and tell me he's sorry, that we can start fresh, that he loves me the way I always dreamed it would be, but then I'd probably lose my friends. My mom and dad would be mad also, especially since they're giving me the money for the attorney, so I guess I'll just fight. I'm going for the house and the kids, for as much as I can. My friends say he deserves to have nothing.

I got served divorce papers this morning. I called her and said it isn't what I want, but she wouldn't change her mind. She agreed to wait to talk to the children until I get home, but I don't think I can do it. It's just about the worst thing we can do to the kids, tearing them apart like this, asking them to take sides, maybe having to sell the family home. Like I said, I begged her, but she said I should have thought about all that before I got involved with another woman. The funny part of it is, I'm not involved with the other woman. Fact is, I just needed someone who liked me so it was easier to come home to someone who didn't. Now I spend my nights alone in the rental. The same thing that got me in trouble in the first place is the last thing I want now. If I never have sex again it'll be fine with me. Look what it's done to our family.

I told him I would wait for him to come home before we told the kids, but I wanted to hurt him by telling them first. I told them everything, even though they're kind of young. I just wanted them to know how rotten he is. I think they should know he cheated on me. Why should I hide it? He should pay for what he's done, and if it means he doesn't have a relationship with the kids, then so be it. In fact, I'm going to do everything I can to make sure he's alone. No more me, no more children. Let's see how happy he is then.

As soon as I walked in the door I knew what Emily had done. The girls were in their rooms crying and Emily was on the telephone with her mother bad-mouthing me. I felt like I let the children down, not because of the affair but because I don't know if they know that I will always love them, that I will always be there for them, that nothing they could ever do, including not speaking to me, will take away the fact that I'm their dad. To tell you the truth, seeing my girls like that, hurt by their mother on purpose, made me want to hit her for the first time in my life. I didn't, but I wished I could have. I tried to talk to her, to ask her to come into the girls' rooms with me and retell the news of the divorce properly, but she laughed right in my face and said, "What's done is done."

My divorce lawyer drew up the paperwork and filed the allegations against Carl. They looked really bad, even to me. The lawyer made him out to be a real lowlife, saying he was a poor provider, a bad husband, and a neglectful father. If anything, Carl has always been twice the parent I've been, but my attorney says if I want to win the case and get the kids, and the child support that goes with them, I have to be ruthless. He asked me to remember times when Carl might have hit me or the kids because that would really ensure winning, but I said I'd have to think about that. When my friends found out about it, they wanted me to make something up about Carl so he would back down. We had a few glasses of wine and by the time the night was over I decided I would give the attorney a little something, not so much that Carl would have to go to jail, but enough that he wouldn't look too good. I feel almost as bad about lying about Carl as I did when I found out about the other woman. Still, my father says, "Take care of business."

Seeing the divorce papers hurt me real bad, but I guess that was Emily's intention. She downright lied about me hurting her and the kids, and accused me of about ten or twelve other things that were stretches of the truth. She said I had never supported her in the manner she should have been taken care of, and that I refused to better myself despite her family's offers of financial and employment assistance. That's a direct quote. The fact of the matter is she means I didn't sell my soul for handouts with strings attached. Emily knows darn well that if anyone has done any hitting in the house it's been her. Every time she loses her temper someone gets a swat across their mouth, more times than I can count. She loves those kids, but there's no way she can take care of them. As it is, she can't set boundaries, she doesn't know how to enforce discipline, so she lets the girls walk all over her. I have a good mind to fight for the girls myself. It's not about the money—hell, money's never meant much to me—but it's about those babies, my girls. They're going to need someone strong to keep things in line as soon as they figure out how important boys are, if the twelve-year-old hasn't figured that out already.

When his attorney counter-filed for divorce, I was stunned, like I was shot with a pistol. He asked for residential custody of the kids. Now you tell me, what man in their right mind is going to ask for custody of two girls? My friends said it sounded kind of kinky, a grown man being that needy to want two young girls living with him, and that got Daddy all fired up. He said if that's what he wants, a fight on his hands, that's what he's going to get.

Emily fired her attorney and hired an out-of-town big-time attorney firm to fight me for custody of the children. I don't want to fight. I don't even want this divorce. I just want to make sure my children are going to be raised safely and with discipline as well as love. Emily is no longer speaking to me at all, and the girls are barely speaking. They tell me their mother said all I wanted to do was tear the family apart and get them so I could keep the child support. My attorney requested a court-ordered forensic psychologist to evaluate the family and make recommendations. I don't know how much all this is going to cost, but I think it's worth the expert opinion no matter what.

I'm resentful that I have to go to the court-ordered forensic psychologist. Why should he have a say in what goes on in my own house? I'm the mother and I think it's ridiculous to assume that anyone can take care of the kids any better than I can. Sure, I think Carl is a great dad, always doing things with the girls, always interested in their schoolwork and visiting their teachers, but I'm not going to tell anyone that. If I do, I'll lose my child support, and I need that money to live. Still, I felt badly making up some of the lies I did in the evaluation, especially in front of the girls. They knew I was lying but they didn't want to go against me, so they just said what I said. I told them later in the car that these were white lies and they didn't count, because I couldn't live without them and they had to do this for me. It seems like the three of us are becoming more and more distant.

The forensic psychologist seemed knowledgeable and was friendly to me and the kids. I wondered how he was ever going to sort this out fairly, especially with the children so aligned with their mother. Oh, don't worry, I know what's going on. I know she's made them tell lies about me, and I don't hold it against them. They're just little girls who are caught in the middle of a big, angry mess and they don't know what to do. Just today I got a call from my younger daughter's teacher relating to conduct problems in the classroom. My girls have never had behavior problems, but this stress has really done a number on all of us. My wife has turned into a blatant liar, I'm a self-proclaimed cheat, and my daughters are struggling to maintain their conduct and their grades. I just tried to answer the psychologist as best I could. No matter how much I might want to fight dirty, I just don't want to get in that muck with Emily. I think she's been a great mother who loves her kids, but not such a great disciplinarian. If the psychologist determines that the kids should go to her, I will abide by that decision. At least I know a professional made the best choice.

I was so mad when I read the psychologist's report. I mean, he saw us as equally good custodial parents and deferred to the judge to make the final determination. I think he saw through my lies about Carl, but he didn't hold it against Carl for the affair. I know the state in which I live doesn't focus on adultery, but someone should. Sure, we both passed the questions about being loving parents, good caretakers, both participating in school and health-related issues, but I want him to lose. I want him to be the big loser.

When the judge awarded residential custodial parenting to Emily with both of us sharing parental responsibility, I have to admit I was relieved. I believe in my heart that the girls need their mother, but I'm still very concerned that she'll be too easy on them and they'll run all over her to get their way. On the way out of the courtroom I told her I was sorry about everything and I wanted us to be friends. She gave me a blank stare and walked away. Maybe it's just too soon for her to forgive me.

When the judge awarded me residential custody, he also ordered the house to be sold. I didn't care, because Daddy bought it and gave Carl half the money, which wasn't much since there was such a huge mortgage. I heard from the girls that Carl got a two-bedroom apartment a few miles away, but I don't care where he lives. The way I see it, the girls and I aren't going to have much to do with him anyway. I told him he could have liberal visitation but I'm going to hold him to the standard state visitation agreement of every other weekend and six weeks in the summer, period. This way he won't be butting into my business and trying to put his two cents in every five seconds about what he thinks the girls should and shouldn't do. I'm going to keep him out of the loop as much as I can. I can't believe that after a year of fighting and mediating, evaluations and testing this day has finally come. I am a free woman. I can't believe I have to answer to no one, that I can do as I please. I also can't believe that I'm not one step closer to getting rid of my anger toward Carl.

The new apartment is tiny, yet it still seems so empty without my family. I call the girls every night, but they're always busy and we really don't catch up much on what they're doing, just the superficial "Hi, how are you? Fine, how about you?" stuff. I asked Emily if I could take them out of state to see my father because he's not doing too well health-wise, but she said no, that it wasn't my weekend. I know the girls would like to see their grandfather before he dies, and it would mean so much to him, but she won't budge. She holds onto that schedule like it was written in cement. She holds me to days and times and will not drop the girls off one minute earlier than she has to. I try to keep busy as much as I can, but I miss my family. I wish I could turn back time.

I'm just frazzled with going back to work and having to deal with these girls. As soon as I walk in the door they've got questions about this and questions about that. They need help with their homework or advice on some boyfriend or other. When I was a kid I figured out how to do my own damn homework. Nobody cares about homework anyway. Just do it as best you can and forget it, that's my advice. All I want to do is take off my shoes, kick back, and watch television with a little peace and quiet. I've got the girls just about every day, and although I wouldn't tell them, I'm pretty sick of it. I know Carl would just love to take them, but that's not going to happen. If I'm on my last breath, I'm not giving him what he wants.

The weekends with the girls just seem to fly by and then they're gone again. I don't like what I'm beginning to see: the way they've been dressing, the excessive makeup, the dyed hair. When I try to speak to Emily about it, she says that's just how girls are, but I'm concerned about the choices they've been making lately. I asked for a family meeting to include Emily but she flat out said no. She said what she does in her house with her kids is none of my business and she'll give me the same respect. It's been over a year and there's no headway made with our communication or friendship. I've done the best I can to be a part of the family, but it's pretty clear that I'm the odd man out. My children are my only salvation. They seem genuinely happy to be with me when I do get to see them. I admit there are many tears shed when they leave.

I'm sick and tired of the attitudes I'm getting from these girls. They seem so happy when they come back from their dad's and then put on the sourpuss face and eye-rolling when they get back into the swing of things at my house. They actually feel sorry for him and call him to make sure he's doing all right. I finally sat them down and told them they are disrespecting me by being loyal to him. "Need I remind you," I said, "that your father is a cheater and the reason we don't have enough money around here?" They got up and marched to their rooms but I stood my ground. I'm not going to slave over their needs and let him get all the accolades. In fact, the trip to Disney they've planned for next weekend isn't going to happen. I don't know how I'm going to stop it but I'll find a way.

I didn't go looking for someone else, but I'm thankful that I found a woman who is as kind and loving as she is. Susan couldn't have children of her own, a fact which pushed her husband away and into a marriage with someone else. Susan is easy to get along with and has a certain reassuring way about her that eases my stress and fills my loneliness. At first I thought it would just be a casual thing, but over the months I've grown to love her. I never thought I would get remarried but I want to spend the rest of my life with her. She's met the girls and seems to get along well with them. She doesn't push herself on them but stays back a little and waits for them to come to her. She has a certain wisdom about things like that, and it makes me happy to see her interact with them.

When the girls told me about Susan, I admit I was jealous and angry. I called Carl and told him under no circumstances did I want my children around any stranger, witnessing who knows what between the two of them. I have a call in to my attorney to stop his visitation if she's present, and at the least I'm going to demand that the girls are not there when she spends the night. He'll probably deny he's sleeping with her, just like he denied the affair. It must be nice to have enough free time to socialize. He's just a waste of a human being. I have a good mind not to take the girls there next weekend. He won't care. He'll probably be relieved that he can devote all his attention to Susan.

I didn't expect Emily to welcome Susan with open arms, but I tried to explain that I didn't let the girls meet her until I knew I was sure about her. It probably wasn't the best timing, but since the subject was already open I told Emily that Susan and I were planning to be married. It will just be my family and a few friends, but I asked Emily if the girls could be part of the wedding party. She had a fit. I didn't want to ask the girls without having their mother prepared first, but they're my children and I'm going to ask them how they feel about participating. I certainly will understand if they think it will cause problems at home and honor their decision to decline, but I do want them to know that no matter how much I love Susan, she will never mean more to me than they do.

My attorney is worthless. He says Carl isn't breaking any laws and if he's going to marry Susan he certainly will have her sleep in the same bed. I spent the past two days locked in my bedroom crying, and I know the girls heard me and I know they know why. They actually want to be in the wedding! They continue to hurt me by their actions. I have a good mind to let them know that if that's all the loyalty they have for me, why don't they pack their stuff up and move in with their dad and Susan. Let's see how long that marriage lasts with the interference of two teenaged kids.

The ceremony was simple and beautiful. Susan made the girls feel so much a part of the celebration and made sure that their hair was done up with flowers. She waited until the last minute, hoping their mother would get them ready and not feel that she was being pushed out of the way, but Emily sent them over like ragamuffins. I have to talk to the girls about their bad grades and some mischief they've been involved in, but I didn't want it to be this weekend. I guess I'll have to wait a couple of weeks before I can sit them down and talk to them face-to-face, since their mother still refuses to allow me access to them on "her weekends." I'm worried about them.

The police knocked on my door at almost two a.m. I was in a sound sleep and when I opened the door I couldn't believe my eyes. There was my oldest daughter leaning on the officer, her clothing a mess and stained with what smelled like vomit. Her eyes were glassed over and her face was red. I can't tell you what he said to me because my brain couldn't absorb his words, but it was something about her sneaking out of the house to meet some boy who lives on the other side of town. They were in a field drinking and who knows what else. The officers brought her home rather than arrest her, but they said she was trespassing, not to mention inebriated. For the first time in years I picked up the telephone and called Carl.

When I heard Emily's voice on the other end of the telephone, screaming and crying, I just prayed no one was dead. When she finally got the words out, I was calm. I think I had been expecting this call for a long time. I rushed over to the house and put our daughter to bed to sleep it off. Emily was in worse shape than she was. I could see the worry in her face, the anger and frustration mixed with overwhelming exhaustion. It was the old Emily I once knew, before her parents planted all the hatred, before her friends riled her up and compounded things. Her hair was disheveled and her makeup was off, but she still looked beautiful to me. Not in a romantic "I wish we were still married" way, but in a "I care about your welfare because we have history and you're the mother of my children" way. She sobbed and blubbered about how she couldn't control the children, how taking them was a mistake, how I was right about her being the worst disciplinarian on the planet. Her words, not mine. She was harder on herself than anything I could have said. She spent the next two hours telling me all the errors she had made with them while I'd been gone and how she didn't know what to do next to gain control of them. I knew it would be easy for me to call my attorney and gain custody, but control was never what it was about for me. What it was always about was the best interest of my children, and when I realized how much she loved and needed these girls I tried to come up with a better solution.

Carl could have taken those girls away from me on the spot. I told him all the things I had been keeping from him. That this wasn't the first time our daughter had sneaked out of the house, that both daughters had been caught drinking and smoking, that one daughter had come back from the doctor with a sexually transmitted disease. Our shared parental responsibility makes it clear that any of those issues must be shared between the parents, but I kept it from him because I didn't want him to think I was a bad mother and because I didn't want to lose my girls. I love them so much and, truthfully, without them I have nothing in my life. All my girlfriends have pretty much gone on to other things. Two moved away, one married for the third time and is in the process of divorcing him, and one got tired of my whining. Instead of pulling out the rug from under me, Carl said we should talk over the next few days and make plans to get our girls on the right track. He said he believes it will take two of us working together for that to happen. He said he respects how much work I've put in with the girls and that despite their behavior problems I've done a good job. I wanted to throw my arms around him and thank him for being so understanding, not in a "I really love you and wish we were still together" way, but in a "Thank you for being my friend and forgiving me for causing you so much pain" way. I slept better that night than I had in years, knowing that I wasn't alone in my responsibilities with the children and that everything was going to be okay.

It took us a good two years before we felt we could trust the girls again, but little by little the family unit began reforming a circle, with one person added so far. Susan has been a big help with the girls and Emily as well. I'm not saying they're friends in the sense that they hang out together, but Emily has come to rely on Susan's objective input from a female perspective. Having never raised children, Susan doesn't have a handle on all the milestones that children go through, but she does have quite a bit of plain old common sense, and she seems to have a good idea of when to butt in and when to butt out. She's not a threat to Emily anymore and, if anything, I think Emily realizes how lonely her life has become without companionship. She asked Susan what she thought about her accepting a date with a man she met working at the bank, and Susan gave her the thumbs up. With one girl in college and one almost there, we've rethought quite a few things. One of them has just about stunned our neighbors and friends. This Thanksgiving Emily invited Susan and me to come for Thanksgiving dinner at her house.

My family thinks I've lost my mind. Maybe I have. My father said that if Carl and his new wife come to Thanksgiving dinner I can expect him to stay home. I felt myself giving in to him, like I did when I was a kid—well, like I did when I was married to

Carl—but instead I got the strength to say what I should have said a long time ago. "I appreciate that you think you know what's best for me, but I need to find my own way. I'm an adult, and I need to do things that, right or wrong, I feel in my heart are right." He backed down. I couldn't believe it. The very next day he called and said, "Your mother and I would very much like to come to your holiday dinner." He didn't even sound like my father. He sounded like a man who was talking to someone he had grown to respect. I sounded confident when I invited everyone, but now that the big day is almost here, I'm a nervous wreck. I don't know what I was thinking, having Carl back in my house, sitting at my table. What will we talk about? Will it be strained? Will it be awful? What if my dinner is a flop? What if she looks beautiful? What if I don't fit in?

The girls are so excited about me and Susan coming for the holiday. They confessed they were sick of pretending to enjoy two turkeys, one at my house and one at Emily's, back to back. I don't know how we're going to pull this off, but we'll try. I'm nervous about going back to my house, remembering where I used to sit in the recliner and read the paper, the porch where I had my morning coffee. Everything has changed, and yet there is a sort of excitement to see all the changes that Emily has made. I've always loved that old place.

Seeing Carl carve the turkey on the same table he used to carve it on, wearing the same flowered apron that I always insisted he wear so he didn't splatter up his shirt, gave me a creepy feeling, like déjà vu—not as bad as I thought I might feel, but not good either. I was thankful my father talked to Carl, and the same with my mother and Susan. It was like I was having some sort of out-of-body experience, sitting in my own home, watching my old husband with his new wife talk to my parents while we passed the potatoes and gravy. The night seemed to take forever, probably because I was always anticipating the worst, even though the time was nothing but pleasant. It was good to see the girls so happy. They weren't frustrated or put out that they had to scarf down their dinner, like in years past, so they could jump to the next meal at the next address. They really seemed happy to see us all together, and I wish I could do this again, but I can't. I really can't. I don't know what I was thinking.

I thought it would be easier than it was. I mean, the company was fine, and Emily did a great job on the dinner. Susan was good company and didn't embarrass anyone by seeming overly "coupled" with me. It was as if we were all just good friends sharing a holiday table, but I have to admit I was sweating. A couple times I wiped my brow and Emily's dad commented on the warm temperatures for this time of the year, but it wasn't the temperature, it was me. I felt like I was going to have a heart attack, worried about whether all the old stuff was going to come up, whether there would be digs about my affair or the divorce, whether Susan would be held up to scrutiny, whether anyone would remember how to make conversation while avoiding all the land mines. The evening couldn't have ended soon enough for me. I told Susan when we got home, "Never again." I just can't put myself through that again. I felt a sense of longing for my house, even though I wouldn't want to live there, and a sense of missing my neighborhood, even though all the neighbors have moved away. I didn't want to be there but I didn't want to leave. It was just too much for me. Never again.

The Christmas season has a way of bringing people together, of goodwill toward men, of needing to be with family. Carl hadn't mentioned anything about all of us spending time together, and neither had I, although we talk a couple times a week, mostly about how we can't believe our children are nearly on their own. Where has the time gone?

Ten days before Christmas I picked up the phone and invited Carl and Susan over to the house for Christmas dinner. Susan said she didn't feel right about me doing the cooking and entertaining and asked about our coming to her house instead. I'm not quite ready for that, but I said perhaps next year. Instead, I asked her if she would make her famous cheese and broccoli casserole that the girls rave so much about. I even bought each of them a gift, not much, just a little something to put under the tree. I don't know if it's the spirit of the season or me coming to the next level of maturity, but I feel suddenly good about having this extended family. Bill, my companion of a couple months, will be yet another addition at the table, and although he doesn't quite understand the dynamics of the new family breaking bread with the old family, he's looking forward to it.

Susan and I bought the girls cashmere sweaters for Christmas and a cashmere scarf and gloves for Emily. I thought it might not be appropriate but Susan insisted, and I think Emily will be surprised to see the package underneath the tree. We brought some candy along with the casserole—white chocolate truffles, because I remember they were always Emily's favorite. It will be strange to see her with someone else, but I'm happy she's found someone she cares about. Driving through the old neighborhood wasn't quite as difficult this time, and as I rang the doorbell I realized there is nowhere else I would rather be than sharing this holiday with my old and new families.

It's been two more Christmases since we all called a silent truce, or should I say since we all agreed to count on each other to be there for the now-grown children. The old adage, "It takes a village to raise a child," has so much more meaning to me now, because I know it's true. Our children are who they have become because of what we gave them through genetics, nurturing, love and good role modeling. When the oldest came home this year sporting an engagement ring, I felt the old panic set in. New territory. I've never been the mother of the bride. Who will I dance with? Who will Carl dance with? Will our daughter dance with her father or Bill or both? How will we ever manage the extravagant wedding she has in mind? It was Carl who said it all: "If we work together, we can make anything happen."

Hi. We know you don't know us, but we're as much a part of this story as Carl and Emily. We're their daughters. We wanted to let you know how important it was to us that our parents finally stopped bickering and fighting, that they stopped pulling us in two different directions and making us feel like we had to choose sides. It made us angry and rebellious to see Mom crying so much and Dad being pushed away from us. We resented her for being so selfish and him for seeming so weak. We wanted them to get back together, but with therapy we realized they weren't happy with each other and that there were too many problems with his infidelity and her dependency on her mother and father. We weren't bad kids, we just got into the wrong crowd and started doing wrong things, kind of keeping pace with other divorced kids who were also angry at their parents for not getting along. Things could have turned out really badly, but when two people love their children enough, they're able to sacrifice their own needs and put the effort into the needs of the kids. That's what our mom and dad did, and it has made all the difference.

Support Groups and Services

Parents undergoing the rigors of divorce need support to prepare themselves for the unexpected and the experience of those who have gone before them, making it through the process successfully. Regardless of how strong a parent is, or how little time is left at the end of the day, devoting yourself to a once/weekly group for support is second only to seeking therapy on an individual basis for assistance with identifying and resolving behaviors within yourself, your spouse and your child. When we are immersed in our own emotional pools, we tend to flail about in deep water without having a clear plan on how to get back to the shallow end. It is this insight that is observed easily by a trained, objective professional, which can guide you back to where you need to be when you find yourself sputtering and sinking.

Websites are particularly popular, hosted by both mental health practitioners and literary authors such as our website **www.InTheBestInterestOfTheChildren.com**, where you will find information about this book and others coming in the future, as well as biographies about the authors.

If you have made it past the initial confusion, or have insight into those pitfalls which can sideswipe even the best laid plans, you might feel better sharing your feelings and emotions with others in a group setting. One of the benefits of groups is that although you believe you are alone, you will come to find that many divorcing individuals share your exact same feelings of anger, despair or anxiety. There will be some groups in which people can come and go, so you will find many stages of divorcing parents in the same room; simply having someone say they have already been where you are now, and they made it through, will help enormously.

Divorce groups can be found in almost every community, and if there is not a support group already set up for divorcing parents, you can set one up yourself. Groups that may fit your needs can be found by checking with your local community centers, religious affiliations and institutions, newspapers and local events, and on-line divorce sites by state.

Finding a group which best suits your needs includes the amount of time you have to commit, as well as whether the particular group you are interested in expects a financial contribution. More often than not, groups which are professionally run, meaning by a mental health practitioner, will have some fees attached, and those fees may have to be paid in advance in one lump sum. As well, there is usually a commitment of time, for example six weeks, in which you will be expected to attend the group weekly for that amount of time. If you are not that organized or do not like to have your time committed to a regular schedule, or if you simply are unable to regulate your time due to children or job constraints, perhaps a different sort of group would better serve your needs.

Groups run by non-professionals are generally self-run, meaning those attending each have equal amounts of time to talk about themselves and their issues, within the time scope of the evening. These groups may or may not have guest speakers, and may or may not ask that your attendance is regular, but generally there will be only a nominal fee for attendance or none at all. Although this type of group may sound ideal for those with time and money difficulties, there are some pitfalls, such as the attendees becoming "stuck" in their own grieving and anger, with the negative atmosphere becoming contagious. Without a professional leader to propel the group forward positively, the sessions may become gripe sessions more than support sessions. The risk of this, of course, is that you will feel hopeless, confused and angry in the end, rather than hopeful and positive that your life will soon be back on track.

A downside to revealing your situation in support groups is that although it is understood that members of the group should not divulge anyone's personal stories outside the group, there are no guarantees that your group members will uphold this confidence. In cities where you are relatively unknown to each other the risk is much less than in smaller communities where you might find your situation repeated when you least expect.

There are also on-line group in which you may register and attend, and these may or may not have financial investments. If you feel more at ease without knowing anyone, and you are able to really speak your thoughts and feelings without inhibition, this may work for you, but if you like the camaraderie of faces and friendliness, of developing possible friendships that spill over from support groups into your personal life, then an on-line group will not be as satisfying overall.

Although the groups in your community will have to be investigated by you, there are on-line group sites found easily by computer. Examples of these on-line groups include:

1) **DivorceRecovery101.com.** This group is very interested in raising happy, successful children as a single parent.

2) **DivorceCare.** This group is available both in the United States and Canada, as well as approximately 15 countries worldwide, and deals with most aspects of divorce.

3) **DC4K.** These initials stand for Divorce Care for Kids, a religiously based organization. It is a ministry for children ages five through twelve years. Many of the leaders of this group have been a product of the divorce process as children, now grown and concerned about the impact in which divorce places on children.

Whether you decide to join an on-line support group or find one in your community, you can be sure that going it alone is never as beneficial as leaning on those who can assist you through this difficult time. There is a group specifically dealing with the needs of single parents and their children called **Parents Without Partners [PWP]**, which has local chapters in the United States and Canada, dealing with topics ranging from coping skills, through the grieving process and beyond.

Some support groups such as **ResponsibleDivorce.com** are gender-based, specifically geared toward men with outreach resources for their girlfriends or second wives. Some groups are geared toward women and some are geared toward single parents with a dating angle. We do not advise these types of dating groups unless you are specifically looking for a date, and not support for divorce and parenting through divorce. There will be time enough for dating later, when the dust settles and you are thinking clearly, which is certainly not during the divorce process. If you're lonely find a good friend, not a bad date.

Lastly on the subject of support groups, there is a wonderful group called **Rainbows**, which is geared specifically for children of divorce, and may be offered at your child's school. Your child's guidance counselor or teacher, who should be kept somewhat aware of your divorce situation so they can watch for unusual behavior signs from your children, will be a good source of information regarding Rainbows. There is usually no charge for this group, and we have found it extremely effective for your youngsters to realize that they are not singled out because of divorce, but rather join a very extensive group of children who are also sad, worried, and having issues which seem much better after an hour or so each week at Rainbows. Rainbows generally has an age group of Kindergarten through age 8, with a younger version called Sunbeams for children ages 3 and 4. In some areas there is another level called Spectrum, dealing with adolescent children of divorce, and Kaleidoscope for college age and young adults.

You can find support without joining a group and guidance without stepping into a therapy office by simply extending yourself to those friends and family who have been there for you in the past. These should be individuals who are non-judgmental, unbiased, kind and compassionate. Often people who would be more than willing to be a shoulder to cry on or an empathetic listener do not want to invade your privacy or overstep their bounds. It is up to you to open the door to their support. Do not use this opportunity to bad-mouth your spouse or air dirty laundry. These support conversations should be more feeling-based or information-seeking than a desire to show your spouse in bad light. It doesn't help in the long run, and once you've divulged personal information which makes juicy gossip, don't be surprised to have it repeated where it doesn't belong.

Another source of support may come in legal form. We are advocates of gathering as much information as you can assimilate while you are contemplating divorce; a very important and often overlooked source of that information comes in the form of family law attorneys who, for a fee, can advise you on your financial circumstances in broad terms so that you can make the best decision for you and your family. They are well-versed in all aspects of family law and divorce, and may be the incentive you need to either leave a bad marriage or repair a good one.

Additional Support Services for Emergencies are your local police department for domestic violence or stalking, reached by dialing 911, or child abuse hot lines, even if abuse is only suspected. The professionals who deal with abuse will make a determination if you legitimately suspect that your child has been abused either physically or sexually. This matter cannot be put off until you are certain. If you believe something happened then it must be investigated. Err on the side of caution. Although many areas have a hotline for reporting child abuse, we hesitate to give these out here, as they may change or may be unreliable in service. Best to call 911 and ask for daytime or nighttime child-abuse numbers for your exact geographic location. A police dispatcher should be able to provide current numbers for such hotlines. You can do this anonymously.

Recommended Reading

More than most any other word, "divorce" elicits everything from war stories to happy endings from friends and strangers alike. However, laced in between facts and accuracy may be well-intended but frightening experiences which may inadvertently lead you astray. Why not consult books specific to divorce and parenting through divorce for factual and informative suggestions and information? Your local library is a good source of up-to-date and tried-and-true divorce books either located in the self-help area or legal area. Often these same libraries may have guest speakers on the subject and your librarian should have a list of monthly events planned for your perusal.

Bookstores, either chain or private, carry a number of books on the subject of divorce and parenting, and again, these may be located in three possible areas including self-help, parenting or legal sections. We have found the following quite useful and reader-friendly:

General Books

1) Ahrons, Constance. *The Good Divorce*. New York: Quill, 1995.

2) Berry, Dawn. *The Divorce Sourcebook*, 3rd Edition. New York: McGraw-Hill, 2007.

3) Clapp, Genevieve. *Divorce and New Beginnings*, 2nd Edition. New York: John Wiley and Sons, Inc., 2000.

4) Cory, Karen. *When Happily Ever After Ends*. Illinois: Sphinx Publishing, 2006.

5) Cruise, Sharon. *Life After Divorce*. Florida: Health Communications, 1994.

6)   Davis, Michele. *Divorce Busting*. New York: Simon and Schuster, 1992.

7)   Davis, Michele. *Divorce Remedy*. New York: Simon and Schuster, 2001.

8)   Freud, Sigmund. *The Interpretation of Dreams*. New York: Barnes and Nobles Classics, 2005.

9)   Gross, James. *Father's Rights*, 2nd Edition. Illinois: Sphinx Publishing, 2006.

10) Krantzler, Mel and Belli, Melvin. *Divorcing*. New York: St. Martin's Griffin, 1988.

11) Margulies, Sam. *Getting Divorced Without Ruining Your Life*. New York: Simon and Schuster, 2001.

12) Neuman, Gary. *Helping Your Kids Cope With Divorce The Sandcastles Way*. New York: Random House, 1998.

13) Peck, M. Scott. *The Road Less Traveled*. New York: Touchstone, 1978.

14) Ricci, Isolina. *Mom's House, Dad's House*. New York: Simon and Schuster, 1980.

15) Sember, Brette. *How To Parent With Your Ex*. Illinois: Sphinx Publishing, 2006.

16) Sember, Brette. *The No Fight Divorce*. New York: McGraw-Hill, 1968.

17) Spence, Gerry. *How To Argue And Win Every Time*. New York: St Martin's Press, 1995.

18) Watnik, Webster. *Child Custody Made Simple*. California: Single Parent Press, 2005.

19) Wild, Russell and Wild, Susan. *The Unofficial Guide To Getting A Divorce*, New Jersey: Wiley Publishing, 2005.

Regardless of which avenue of support you choose, remember that information and support are only a phone call, website, or bookstore away so take advantage of as many channels as you can to smooth both your emotions and the process when dealing with divorce and parenting.

Index

clothing, 74–75
communication, 10–11, 36–39
  between adults when children are present, 2, 14–15. *See also under* parents modes of, 39
consistency, need for, 11–13. *See also* discipline
custody battles, 42–51, 89–91
  children testifying in, 46–47

D

dating and new relationships, 49, 68–71
dating groups, 117
DC4K, 116
depositions, 58–60
depression, 7
discipline, 11–13, 25–28
dishonesty, 27
divorce, 1–2, 4. *See also specific topics*
  case study, 92–113
  filing for, 52, 53, 56
  meanings of the word, 22
  as nasty business, 16–18
Divorce Care for Kids (DC4K), 116
divorce groups, 115
DivorceCare.com, 116
DivorceRecovery101.com, 116
domestic violence, 77–83, 118
drug abuse, 68

E

e-mail, 39
emergency services, 118

F

financial issues, 9, 55–58, 61–62, 74–76. *See also* attorneys
legal fees, 52–54
food, 76
forensic psychologists, 43–46, 89

G

gender roles, 23–24, 31–32

H

health, child, 72–73
honesty, 27
house, clean, 73–74
humor, 11

I

illness in children, 72–73
impulsiveness, 24
incest, 84–88
instant gratification, 24
Internal Revenue Service (IRS), 57–58
interrogatories, 56–57

L

language, 37. *See also* communication
lawyers. *See* attorneys
limit setting, 11. *See also* discipline

Other Titles of Interest from Hohm Press

CONSCIOUS PARENTING
by Lee Lozowick

Any individual who cares for children needs to attend to the essential message of this book: that the first two years are the most crucial time in a child's education and development, and that children learn to be healthy and "whole" by living with healthy, whole adults.

Offers practical guidance and help for anyone who wishes to bring greater consciousness to every aspect of childraising, including: * conception, pregnancy and birth* emotional development * language usage * role modeling: the mother's role, the father's role * the exposure to various influences * establishing workable boundaries * the choices we make on behalf on our children's education ... and much more.

Paper, 378 pages, formerly $17.95   ISBN: 0-934252-67-X
Available at a reduced price as publisher's seconds only

THE WAY OF FAILURE: *Winning Through Losing*
by Mariana Caplan

This straight-talking and strongly inspirational book looks failure directly in the face, unmasking it for what it really is. Mariana Caplan tells us to how to meet failure on its own field, how to learn its twists and turns, its illusions and its realities. Only then, she advises, is one equipped to engage failure as a means of ultimate "winning," and in a way that far exceeds our culturally defined visions of success.

Paper, 144 pages, $14.95   ISBN: 1-890772-10-6

To Order: 800-381-2700, or visit our website, www.hohmpress.com

THE JUMP INTO LIFE
Moving Beyond Fear
by Arnaud Desjardins
Foreword by Richard Moss, M.D.

"Say *Yes* to life," the author continually invites in this welcome guidebook to the spiritual path. For anyone who has ever felt oppressed by the life-negative seriousness of religion, this book is a timely antidote. In language that translates the complex to the obvious, Desjardins applies his simple teaching of happiness and gratitude to a broad range of weighty topics, including sexuality and intimate relationships, structuring an "inner life," the relief of suffering, and overcoming fear.

Paper, 278 pages, $12.95   ISBN: 0-934252-42-4

THE ACTIVE CREATIVE CHILD
Parenting in Perpetual Motion
by Stephanie Vlahov

Active/creative children are often misunderstood by the medical community, by schools, and by their own parents. Their energy is astounding; their inquisitiveness is boundless. Channeling that energy is not only helpful, but necessary. Supporting that inquisitiveness is essential! This book provides specific hints for coping, for establishing realistic boundaries, for avoiding labels and easy judgments where any child is concerned. Written in a simple, journalistic style, the author draws from her experience with her two active/creative sons, and those of others, to present a handbook of encouragement and genuine help

Paper, 105 pages, $9.95   ISBN: 1-890772-47-X

To Order: 800-381-2700, or visit our website, www.hohmpress.com

TO TOUCH IS TO LIVE
The Need for Genuine Affection in an Impersonal World
by Mariana Caplan
Foreword by Ashley Montagu

The vastly impersonal nature of contemporary culture, supported by massive child abuse and neglect, and reinforced by growing techno-fascination are robbing us of our humanity. The author takes issue with the trends of the day that are mostly overlooked as being "progressive" or harmless, showing how these trends are actually undermining genuine affection and love. This uncompromising and inspiring work offers positive solutions for countering the effects of the growing depersonalization of our times.

"An important book that brings to the forefront the fundamentals of a healthy world. We must all touch more." – Patch Adams, M.D.

Paper, 272 pages, $19.95   ISBN: 1-890772-24-0

THE WAY OF POWER
by RedHawk

RedHawk's poetry cuts close to the bone whether he is telling humorous tales or indicting the status-quo throughout the culture. Touching upon themes of life and death, power, devotion and adoration, these eighty new poems reveal the poet's deep concern for all of life, and particularly for the needs of women, children and the earth

"This is such a strong book. RedHawk is like Whitman: he says what he sees..." – the late William Packard, former editor, *New York Quarterly*.

Paper, 96 pages, $10.00   ISBN: 0-934252-64-5

To Order: 800-381-2700, or visit our website, www.hohmpress.com

AFTER SURGERY, ILLNESS, OR TRAUMA
10 Practical Steps to Renewed Energy and Health
by Regina Sara Ryan,
Foreword by John W. Travis, M.D.

This book fills the important need of helping us survive and even thrive through our necessary "down-time" in recuperating from surgery, trauma, or illness. Whether you are recovering at home or in the hospital for a few days, weeks, or even months, this book will be your guide to a more balanced and even productive recovery. It follows a wellness-approach that addresses: managing and reducing pain; coping with fear, anger, frustration and other unexpected emotions; inspiration for renewed life, becoming an active participant in your own healing; dealing with well-meaning visitors and caregivers...and more.

Paper, 285 pages, $14.95   ISBN: 0-934252-95-5

10 ESSENTIAL FOODS
by Lalitha Thomas

Carrots, broccoli, almonds, grapefruit and six other miracle foods will enhance your health when used regularly and wisely. Lalitha gives in-depth nutritional information plus flamboyant and good-humored stories about these foods, based on her years of health and nutrition counseling. Each chapter contains easy and delicious recipes, tips for feeding children and helpful hints for managing your food dollar. A bonus section supports the use of *10 Essential Snacks*.

"Bravo! This book details 10 of the most important foods you need to grow and maintain a healthy, vital body." – Dr. Michael Colgan, author, *Optimum Sports Nutrition.*

Paper, 300 pages, $16.95   ISBN: 0-934252-74-2

To Order: 800-381-2700, or visit our website, www.hohmpress.com

PARENTING, A SACRED TASK
10 Basics of Conscious Childraising
by Karuna Fedorschak

Moving beyond our own self-centered focus and into the realm of generosity and expansive love is the core of spiritual practice. This book can help us to make that move. It highlights 10 basic elements that every parent can use to meet the everyday demands of childraising. Turning that natural duty into a sacred task is what this book is about. Topics include: love, attention, boundaries, food, touch, help and humor.

"There is no more rigorous path to spiritual development than that of being a parent. Thank you to Karuna Fedorschak for remind us that parenting is a sacred task." – Peggy O'Mara, Editor and Publisher, *Mothering Magazine*.

Paper, 158 pages, $12.95   ISBN: 1-890772-30-5

ROSIE, THE SHOPPING-CART LADY
by Chia Martin with Illustrations by Jewel Hernandez

This children's picture book tells what happens when a sensitive little boy confronts the hard reality of a disheveled old woman who wanders the city streets collecting trash or treasures in her shopping cart. It addresses neither the global questions of injustice nor a specific solution to the massive problem of homelessness in the U.S. today. Rather, easy-rhyming text and colorful illustrations highlight a story designed to inspire questions and conversation about this important subject.

"This heartwarming story is a reminder of the need for each of us to become involved in our communities. It is never too early to learn the message contained in *Rosie*. – Elaine L. Chao, President and CEO, United Way of America

Hardcover, 32 pages; 16 illustrations, $15.95 ISBN: 0-934252-52-2

To Order: 800-381-2700, or visit our website, www.hohmpress.com

THE ALCHEMY OF TRANSFORMATION
by Lee Lozowick
Foreword by: Claudio Naranjo, M.D.

A concise and straightforward overview of the principles of spiritual life as developed and taught by Lee Lozowick for the past twenty years. Subjects of use to seekers and serious students of any spiritual tradition include: A radical, elegant and irreverent approach to the possibility of change from ego-centeredness to God-centeredness--the ultimate human transformation .

Paper, 185 pages, $14.95   ISBN: 0-934252-62-9

THE SHADOW ON THE PATH
Clearing the Psychological Blocks to Spiritual Development
by VJ Fedorschak
Foreword by Claudio Naranjo, M.D.

Tracing the development of the human psychological shadow from Freud to the present, this readable analysis presents five contemporary approaches to spiritual psychotherapy for those who find themselves needing help on the spiritual path. Offers insight into the phenomenon of denial and projection.
    Topics include: the shadow in the Work; notable therapists; the principles of inner spiritual development in the major world religions; examples of the disowned shadow in contemporary religious movements; and case studies of clients in spiritual groups who have worked with their shadow issues.

Paper, 300 pages, $17.95   ISBN: 0-934252-81-5

To Order: 800-381-2700, or visit our website, www.hohmpress.com

THE ANTI-WISDOM MANUAL
Ways and Means to Fail on the Spiritual Path
by Gilles Farcet, Ph.D.

What if the spiritual path turned out to be a road to hell paved with good intentions?

Most spiritual books tell us what we *should* do, or how we *should* view things. *The Anti-Wisdom Manual* takes a different approach. It simply describes what people *actually do* to sabotage their own progress on the spiritual path, whatever their chosen way – Christian, Buddhist, Native American, Muslim, Jewish, or any other. Think of it as a handbook in reverse. Using humor and irony, while based in clarity and compassion, the author alerts readers to the common traps into which so many sincere seekers easily fall.

Paper, 176 pages, $14.95   ISBN: 1-890772-42-9

BEYOND ASPIRIN
Nature's Challenge To Arthritis, Cancer & Alzheimer's Disease
by Thomas A. Newmark and Paul Schulick

A reader-friendly guide to one of the most remarkable medical breakthroughs of our times. Research shows that inhibition of the COX-2 enzyme significantly reduces the inflammation that is currently linked with arthritis, colon and other cancers, and Alzheimer's disease. Challenging the conventional pharmaceutical "silver-bullet" approach, this book pleads a convincing case for the safe and effective use of the COX-2-inhibiting herbs, including green tea, rosemary, basil, ginger, turmeric and others.

Paper, 340 pages, $14.95   ISBN: 0-934252-82-3
Cloth; 340 pages, $24.95   ISBN: 1-890772-01-1

To Order: 800-381-2700, or visit our website, www.hohmpress.com

THE ALCHEMY OF LOVE AND SEX
by Lee Lozowick
Foreword by Georg Feuerstein, Ph.D.

Reveals 70 "secrets" about love, sex and relationships. Lozowick recognizes the immense conflict and confusion surrounding love, sex, and tantric spiritual practice. Advocating neither asceticism nor hedonism, he presents a middle path—one grounded in the appreciation of simple human relatedness. Topics include:* what men want from women in sex, and what women want from men * the development of a passionate love affair with life * how to balance the essential masculine and essential feminine * the dangers and possibilities of sexual Tantra * the reality of a genuine, sacred marriage. . .and much more.

" ... attacks Western sexuality with a vengeance." – *Library Journal.*

Paper, 300 pages, $16.95   ISBN: 0-934252-58-0

KISHIDO: *The Way of the Western Warrior*
by Peter Hobart

The code of the samurai and the path of the knight-warrior – traditions from opposite sides of the globe – find a common ground in *Kishido: the Way of the Western Warrior*. In fifty short essays, Peter Hobart presents the wisdom, philosophy and teachings of the mysterious Master who first united the noble houses of East and West. Kishido prioritizes the ideals of duty, ethics, courtesy and chivalry, from whatever source they derive. This cross-cultural approach represents a return to time-honored principles from many traditions, and allows the modern reader from virtually any background to find the master within.

Paper, 130 pages, $12.95   ISBN: 1-890772-31-3

To Order: 800-381-2700, or visit our website, www.hohmpress.com

YOU HAVE THE RIGHT TO REMAIN SILENT
Bringing Meditation to Life
by Rick Lewis

With sparkling clarity and humor, Rick Lewis explains exactly what meditation can offer to those who are ready to establish an island of sanity in the midst of an active life. This book is a comprehensive look at everything a beginner would need to start a meditation practice, including how to befriend an overactive mind and how to bring the fruits of meditation into all aspects of daily life. Experienced meditators will also find refreshing perspectives to both nourish and refine their practice.

Paper, 201 pages, $14.95   ISBN: 1-890772-23-2

YOGA FROM THE INSIDE OUT
Making Peace with Your Body through Yoga
by Christina Sell

This book is about Yoga and body image. It is about the journey from various addictions and self-hatred into self-acceptance leading to spiritual practice. It is based in the principles of Anusara Yoga, a style of hatha yoga that integrates physical practice with inner body awareness and a deep connection to the heart. Christina Sell is a certified instructor of Anusara Yoga. In her own life and those of her friends and students, she has seen the devastating effects of the war against the body.

"Christina reminds us that practicing yoga is so much more than just postures and breathing. It is a deeply personal journey back home to ourselves, and it takes us from self-doubt and judgment to self-acceptance and joy."
                                                        – Judith Hanson Lasater, Ph.D.

Paper, 144 pages, b&w photos, $14.95   ISBN: 1-890772-32-1

To Order: 800-381-2700, or visit our website, www.hohmpress.com

About the Authors

Nadir Baksh, Psy.D. is a Licensed Clinical Psychologist specializing in Clinical and Forensic Psychology since 1984. He is a Fellow of the American Association of Integrative Medicine and the American Board of Forensic Examiners, with over twenty-two years of clinical experience in office practice. Dr. Baksh is considered an expert in court testimony, and has worked for twenty years in child custody evaluations and marital therapy. He sees first hand the effects of separation and divorce on the individuals in the relationship, especially the children.

Laurie Elizabeth Murphy, R.N., Ph.D. has raised four children. Since the beginning of her training in 1968 she has worked with patients and families. For the past twenty years she has specifically focused on a clinical practice dealing with marital issues, divorce and its impact on children.

Contact Information

Laurie Murphy and Nadir Baksh have an active website. Please visit them at www.InTheBestInterestOfTheChildren.com. Use the *Contact Us* section on the website to send your questions, and they will try to answer as many as possible. They also love comments from readers. Send correspondence to 421 Martin Avenue, Stuart, Florida 34996.